MW00810254

THE **CQ** EDGE

||||||||| SU BRIDGMAN |||||||||

THE

EDGE

HOW TO **IGNITE CONFIDENCE,**

ELIMINATE ANXIETY AND MAXIMIZE YOUR

COMMUNICATION INTELLIGENCE

Forbes | Books

Published by Forbes Books, Charleston, South Carolina.
An imprint of Advantage Media Group.

Forbes Books is a registered trademark, and the Forbes Books colophon is a trademark of Forbes Media, LLC.

Printed in the United States of America.

10 9 8 7 6 5 4 3 2 1

ISBN: 979-8-88750-156-7 (Hardcover)
ISBN: 979-8-88750-157-4 (eBook)

Library of Congress Control Number: 2024900712

Cover and layout design by Matthew Morse.

This custom publication is intended to provide accurate information and the opinions of the author in regard to the subject matter covered. It is sold with the understanding that the publisher, Forbes Books, is not engaged in rendering legal, financial, or professional services of any kind. If legal advice or other expert assistance is required, the reader is advised to seek the services of a competent professional.

Since 1917, Forbes has remained steadfast in its mission to serve as the defining voice of entrepreneurial capitalism. Forbes Books, launched in 2016 through a partnership with Advantage Media, furthers that aim by helping business and thought leaders bring their stories, passion, and knowledge to the forefront in custom books. Opinions expressed by Forbes Books authors are their own. To be considered for publication, please visit **books.Forbes.com**.

DEDICATION

This book is lovingly dedicated to the pillars of my life and the many voices that have echoed through the corridors of my journey, each playing a vital role in shaping my understanding of communication and the power of voice.

To my father and mother, my grit gurus, who instilled in me the resilience and tenacity that underpin every word I write. Your unwavering strength and wisdom have been my guiding lights, teaching me the value of persistence and the beauty of articulating one's thoughts with clarity and conviction.

To my clients, who have placed their trust in me, you have been the inspiration for refining the strategies within these pages. Your journeys, challenges, and successes have kept the pilot light burning in my quest to help individuals maximize their potential daily. Your faith in me has been a driving force, continually fueling my passion to explore and expand the boundaries of effective communication.

To my four daughters, Maya, Karma, Aishwarya, and Xia, who reinforce every day my commitment to the power of voice. You remind me that our words can shape our realities, and through them we can inspire, heal, and empower. Your curiosity, intelligence, and compassion are the greatest testaments to the potency of effective communication.

To my husband, my steadfast supporter and confidant, thank you for your encouragement and belief in my abilities. Your support has been a constant source of strength and motivation.

To my sisters, Sumita, Charlie, Tania, and Namrata, whose feedback, design eye, and unwavering support over the years have been indispensable. Your insights and perspectives have enriched not only the content but also the presentation of this book. Your knack for objective feedback, coupled with an unerring sense of aesthetics, has been instrumental in bringing the pages of this book to life.

And most importantly to Joshin, whose encouragement to share my knowledge and experiences in the form of this book has been invaluable. Your guidance and enthusiasm have been a beacon, guiding me through the process of transforming thoughts and teachings into the pages you hold.

This book is not just a compilation of my insights, but a celebration of the voices and influences that have shaped me. May it serve as a testament to the power of communication in connecting, understanding, and elevating one another.

With profound gratitude,
Su

DEAR READER,

Welcome to this transformative journey toward developing your communication intelligence, finding your true voice, and unlocking your full potential while eliminating anxiety. I am grateful and honored that you have chosen to embark on this path with me.

In these pages, we will explore science-backed strategies and techniques that can empower you to communicate with confidence, authenticity, and impact. The goal is to equip you with the tools and insights necessary to navigate both personal and professional interactions with clarity and conviction.

Throughout this book, my intention is to provide practical guidance, share knowledge, and inspire you to embrace your unique strengths and abilities. I firmly believe that each person possesses untapped potential, waiting to be unleashed through effective communication.

I have poured my passion and dedication into crafting these pages, drawing upon my own experiences, research, and the wisdom of others. But I want to acknowledge that this journey would not be possible without you, the reader. Your willingness to explore these ideas and apply them in your own life is what makes this journey worthwhile.

I extend my deepest gratitude to you for joining me on this quest for personal growth, self-awareness, self-discovery, and enhanced communication skills. Together, let us embrace the transformative power of communication intelligence, find our confidence, and unleash our true voices.

I wish you an insightful journey as you "CQ with Su"!

Contents

About the Author 1

Introduction 3

CHAPTER 1
What Is CQ, and Why Do You Need to Master It? 17

CHAPTER 2
Mastering CQ through Vocal Image Transformation 35

CHAPTER 3
Positive Psychology and the CQ Mindset. 55

CHAPTER 4
The Science behind Vocal Image 81

CHAPTER 5
The Physiology of Voice 99

CHAPTER 6
Cortisol and Stress—How to Control Them 109

CHAPTER 7

From Grit to Gravitas **139**

CHAPTER 8

Your CQ Checklist—Content **153**

CHAPTER 9

Your CQ Checklist—Vocal Impact **195**

CHAPTER 10

Your CQ Checklist—Nonverbal Communication. **215**

CHAPTER 11

Next Step—Find Your Safe Place. **243**

About the Author

Su Bridgman, JD, inspires professionals, executives, and CEOs to maximize their potential with SpeakFluence—to *speak with influence* and *lead with impact*.

With her background as a commercial litigator and passion for psychology, and as the founder of SpeakFluence Global, Su has been selected by Forbes Books as the international authority on communication intelligence and as Forbes's communication industry specialist. Su is disrupting the traditional belief that one's fear of public or social speaking situations or of asserting one's persuasive self is a fixed state or a diagnosed syndrome.

Su's mission is to support clients to achieve communication flow—that is, the ability to access communication intelligence as required, on demand, while embracing and retaining one's innate personality. Using her science-based methodology, she partners with both the education industry and innovative forward-thinking international organizations to transform their ethos and empower executives to align their vocal images with their corporate brands to nurture twenty-first-century success skills.

As one of the earliest MENA regional representatives of the Education Division of the International Positive Psychology Association, Su advocated for the need to integrate and promote positive psychology and neuroscience research in the educational and corporate landscapes in the MENA region. Through her charitable work with organizations such as Educate Girls Globally, she has empowered underprivileged young women to find their voices, obtain access to education, and shift their mindsets to become future leaders through the development of girls' parliaments and positive-psychology-rooted methodology. Her passion for servant leadership is clear through her numerous board positions with Young Presidents' Organization (YPO), where she has curated future readying learning programs. She was twice awarded the Global Award, by both YPO MENA and YPO International, for Best Full Family Program and Best Spouse/Partner Full Program across 450 chapters globally. Su has served on the YPO Dubai Board, the Middle East North Africa Regional Executive Board, and the Parenting Network of the Young Presidents' Organization.

Introduction

What if I told you that you could share the brilliance of your mind with any audience, at the drop of the proverbial hat, void of any anxiety, nervousness, or physiological response? That's what I help people achieve. Communication intelligence. CQ. Whoever you are, whatever your message and your goal, communication intelligence will transform your speaking and your life.

Contrary to the traditional belief that one's communication ability (or inability) is a fixed state, the methods I will present in the following pages hinge on the notion that we each have an amazing capacity for transformation. As you work through this book, you will learn how to overhaul your communication style and habits—just as my clients do—through a combined mastery of the *science of speaking* and *psychology*. This journey will teach you to "self-hack" through self-awareness, mindful intention, and a focused, gritty approach to developing your confidence and mastery of communication skills.

"But what about fear?" you ask.

Or perhaps you respond with one of these comments:

- "I hate speaking in public."
- "I'm a terrible speaker."
- "I get too nervous in front of people."
- "Soft skills? It's just fluff—I am a technically strong professional, and that is all that matters."
- "I'm fine until I think about being judged by everyone around the boardroom table."
- "I have never been a good communicator. It's just not my strength."
- "I am not like the typical extrovert who can wow a crowd or schmooze a room—it's just not me."
- "I start off strong and get nervous when I see people are starting to lose interest in what I am saying."
- "I can't get my words out. My heart throbs; my knees feel weak. I get a lump in my throat; I lose all train of thought."
- "I have always been quiet. I don't think people value what I have to say."
- "I know my stuff. I just can't get it across to my superiors."
- "I'm the most experienced on the team but never 'heard' by my superiors."

And one of the most common self-labels: "But I'm an introvert."

I have heard these and similar statements repeatedly from clients over the past decade. They earnestly believe that their communication abilities are fixed and that they were either born or had life experiences that have created limitations within them with respect to their communication skill.

Many people refer to them as excuses. I believe this is insensitive and inaccurate, given how personal this skill is. If any one of these mindsets has crossed your mind, I invite you to take your very important first step this moment and shift your language. Shift to the belief that this phrase or collection of words is merely a mindset that is driving you. In fact, it is these types of mindsets that hold people back from achieving their peak communication performance.

By the time you finish this book, you won't let any of these inner messages keep you from communicating with all the power you possess. That's not to deny that one or more of those mindsets may be your reality right now. Glossophobia, or the fear of public speaking, is one of our society's most widely documented phobias. According to the National Social Anxiety Center, "The fear of public speaking is the most common phobia ahead of heights, spiders, and death."[1]

Do remember, though, the definition of *phobia*: "an extreme or irrational fear of or aversion to something." Synonyms include terms like *abnormal fear*, *irrational fear*, *obsessive fear*, *dislike*, and *distaste*. All of these are temporary states, as is glossophobia, when you have the tools to eradicate their causes or empower you to shift your perspective to one that is within your control.

Most of us have experienced moments when we question our ability to translate what is in our heads—both the messages we wish to deliver and the effectiveness with which we wish to deliver them—into reality. When this happens, we are really questioning our ability to communicate with impact. Ultimately, we are questioning our CQ. This book will teach you how to push through these stressful moments of self-doubt as you develop awareness of your physiology.

Inherent in mastering communication intelligence is the understanding that you have a remarkable degree of control over the physical

---

1   John Montopoli, "Public Speaking Anxiety and Fear of Brain Freezes," National Social Anxiety Center, February 20, 2017, https://nationalsocialanxietycenter. com/2017/02/20/public-speaking-and-fear-of-brain-freezes/.

responses frequently triggered by high-stakes or high-pressure speaking events and situations. It is those physical responses that impact how (and the success with which) you share the content and message you know so well and whether you are impactful and memorable. The heart of this book consists of a series of exercises I use successfully with my own clients, be they beginning student speakers or high-level CEOs. These exercises integrate the neuroscience of communication, and combined with the six-week journal at the end of the book, they will help you develop your CQ, starting the very first week.

FLOW: WHAT YOU'LL ACHIEVE BY MASTERING YOUR COMMUNICATION INTELLIGENCE

If you are to feel and be perceived as a strong communicator, you're going to need the tools contained in this book. First, you'll need the grit that motivates you to practice the tools. Then, as you master communication intelligence, you'll achieve a state of flow similar to the psychological state referenced in Mihaly Csikszentmihalyi's groundbreaking book *Flow: The Psychology of Optimal Experience.*[2] When it comes to communication, flow is the ability to consistently self-correct—in the moment—and ensure an impactful and memorable impression, unhindered by the physiological triggers that derail even the best-prepared presentations and speeches. One is in a flow state when they are in a state of intense concentration. Their thoughts are focused on an experience rather than on themselves, they lose a sense of time and feel as if there is a merging of their actions and awareness. This is balanced by their skill so that they are fully involved in the present moment. Some refer to this as being "in the zone." These expe-

---

2   Mihaly Csikszentmihalyi, *Flow: The Psychology of Optimal Experience* (New York: Harper Perennial Modern Classics, 2008).

riences are intrinsically rewarding and one has complete awareness and control throughout.

Use this book to remove your personal limits and labels while becoming a naturally authentic communicator. Learn how to switch on the ability to speak with confidence and charisma when necessary—without attempting to change your personality.

Step by step, you will learn how to achieve a communication growth mindset through practical exercises that help put your ideas into action. You will examine the challenges presented by the fixed mindset and explore how your internal dialogue impacts your confidence and ability to develop communication skills. You will learn how to tap into the strengths-based character development of positive psychology to shed limitations imposed by labels you previously accepted for yourself.

WHY THE TWENTY-FIRST-CENTURY HUMAN WORKFORCE IS DEFINED BY COMMUNICATION

As our technology improves, hard skills (those abilities that can be defined, measured, and programmed) are becoming increasingly mechanized. Meanwhile, soft skills—those less tangible human qualities such as empathy, humility, and the ability to emotionally connect with an audience—are in growing demand.[3]

I often think of my early days as a junior lawyer, sitting in a boardroom for the entire summer and reviewing documents, putting sticky tabs on certain pages to identify whether they were relevant. Was that a great learning experience? In a special way, I suppose; at

---

3   Paul Thagard, cognitive scientist and author of the *Treatise on Mind and Society* collection, says, "On the theory that emotions are physiological perceptions, robots will probably never have human emotions, because they will never have human bodies. It might be possible to simulate physiological inputs, but the complexity of the signals that people get from all of their organs makes this unlikely." https://www. psychologytoday.com/us/blog/hot-thought/201712/will-robots-ever-have-emotions.

least, so I thought at the time. I remember thinking at the time of all the critical thinking skills required.

Software has revolutionized work efficiency and cost-effectiveness, dramatically reshaping the landscape of traditional practices. Take the case of young lawyers: no longer do they wade through a sea of documents with sticky tabs. This shift mirrors the ongoing evolution of the global workforce.

Artificial intelligence (AI) has become a powerful influence, with generative AI like GPT-4 seizing the spotlight in the news. In this brave new world, our personal currency is our ability to communicate. Yet the pandemic has challenged our communication capabilities profoundly, from remote work dynamics to the rise of online education.

The younger generation stands at the epicenter of this shift. Stripped of crucial developmental time, they grapple with communication and social skills, their lives increasingly intertwined with technology and online platforms. As we watch this narrative unfold, it's clear that the global implications will be substantial.

Amid this turmoil, the pandemic has also fueled a surge in technology use across all generations, altering our capacity for communication. As AI continues to mature, it presents us with tremendous opportunities: gateways to pursue our passions, optimize our time, and augment the collective human knowledge.

The world of consulting offers a striking illustration. My clients are investing in the growth of their employees' soft skills, preparing them for a future where client-facing roles take precedence. With the relentless advance of AI, many "technical skills" are becoming obsolete, replaced by the intelligent systems that are reshaping the fabric of our workforce.

The major area in which AI cannot supplant human talent is, appropriately enough, humanness. The arena of communication skills is still the jurisdiction of human beings, and as such, it is increasingly important and a key skill to harness to be competitive. When we're able to overcome our communication limitations and maximize our abilities, we're not simply enhancing our self-validation in a casual or vague way. We are securing our vitality and relevance in a twenty-first-century world; communication intelligence is the future personal currency that contributes to success.

THE EFFECT OF A PANDEMIC ON COMMUNICATION

This book was originally written before the COVID-19 pandemic. I could not help but update it, given the complete disruption to the global workforce, home, and schools. Digital technology was a lifeline during the COVID-19 crisis. It made work and connection in many domains possible, allowing over 1.4 billion children to remain "in school," but it did so in ways that were "often intrusive, exhausting, and potentially corrosive to face-to-face relationships."[4] Schools are also observing the long-term social impact students are experiencing because of the loss of face-to-face communication due to masks and online learning during the formative periods. An entire generation has been impacted, and it is yet to be seen how this will affect their futures. It also catapulted the world into a situation in which professionals had a new skill to harness—online impression management.

What was once a world where people communicated in a most human form—in person—surreally transformed into one where Zoom, Teams, Google Meet, and other videoconferencing "meetings" became the norm and essential to maintain business and the economy.

---

4   https://www.fastcompany.com/90491367/
     screens-are-lifesavers-right-now-but-theyre-still-relationship-wreckers.

Firms and organizations had to rely upon their employees to learn to communicate in what was, for many, a foreign manner. Overnight, individuals had to learn to adapt to a new form of "communication," with limited or no guidance, with no runway to prepare for the new reality. Partners at professional firms have seen the negative impact videoconferencing has had on team connectivity, the lack of motivation and energy in calls, and the blank faces that were once gleaming with innovation and drive.

While, for some, the screen has become a protective shield from people who might otherwise have been intimidating (resulting in a confidence boost), for others it has become a major challenge, as they are not comfortable onscreen, and this may cause additional anxiety. Due to the higher cognitive demands that videoconferencing places on viewers, attendees in videoconferences tend to be more influenced by heuristic judgmental cues than they are by the quality of the content presented by the speaker.[5]

The screen has become a mirror that the mind is constantly scanning for others' reactions to what we are saying. This has resulted in videoconference fatigue for many, but more importantly, it can be challenging to be heard, maintain audience attention, and recreate meaningful connection. Such communication difficulties can cause our brains to release cortisol,[6] which you'll read more about later.

In addition, this has nixed a huge component of our communication message—much of our nonverbal communication and behaviors—which, as we will learn later, are key to making an impact

5   Carlos Ferran and Stephanie Watts Sussman, "Videoconferencing in the Field: A Heuristic Processing Model," *Management Science* 54, no. 9 (September 2008): 1565–1578, https://www.researchgate.net/publication/220534937_Videoconfferencing_in_the_Field_A_Heuristic_Processing_Model.

6   https://www.linkedin.com/pulse/affects-positive-negative-communication-martin-johnson/.

on our audience. They often speak louder than words and comprise over 50 percent of your communication message—put simply, we must mind our microexpressions! Your gestures, posture, and tone of voice, and the way you make eye contact, send strong messages. They can put people at ease, build trust, and draw others toward you. They can also offend, confuse, and undermine what you're trying to convey!

Nonverbal communication is incredibly important for businesses, from interacting with customers to negotiating with vendors, building trust to launch campaigns, and coordinating efforts between employees. Body language plays a significant role in deciding the fate of any video-conference. It's hard to build the same trust one achieves with face-to-face communication. When you can't see the person you are talking to, you are missing out on important social signals including affirmation, assurance, agreement, empathy, doubt, confidence, and lack of clarity.

From a leadership perspective, building trust through one's communication is always important to develop confidence in one's community or organization, but it is even more important in a crisis situation. Leaders were called upon to, overnight, manage their personal anxieties/worries while concurrently kindling an elevated self-awareness within themselves that would inspire vision and hope within their organizations.

There was much discussion in the corporate arena about the missing "human factor" during the COVID-19 crisis. On Zoom calls, leaders had to keep in mind that no one could see their body language, and they couldn't see the body language of their audiences. Without the visual cues of body language, words and vocal nuances are even more important in all our interactions.

I believe that this crisis will continue to remind us all how "humanness" is so key to connection; the screen removes our ability to interact despite the human need for touch. I believe it will show us that in a new world, there may be a need to reenvision communication in the future. There will likely be an increased importance on "displaying" candor, vulnerability, and transparency through both tone and language choice. There may need to be a refocus of both content and the ability to inspire confidence through a leadership vision that promotes resilience and perseverance. While organizations to date have been creative in making the best of this, it is expected to take a major toll on the mental health and well-being of workers, adding a layer of concern for leaders who will need to reignite the corporate culture from a distance.

It will require a new skill set through which a person will need to make a fantastic "virtual first impression" to be hired—and somehow overcome the fact that humans instinctively look for heuristic cues to form judgments. It may in some ways be "virtually perfect" for those who feel intimidated by others who are physically more imposing, louder, or more boisterous, allowing them to finally speak their brilliance and be heard. It may, in some way, level the playing field from a gender perspective, and it may also be beneficial, as one's self-awareness, authenticity, vulnerability, and intrinsic self-talk are positive traits that actually increase one's virtual presence and ability to connect quicker, void of any external factors on how a corporate meeting unfolds. It will be interesting to see the impacts of COVID-19-induced virtual workplace settings and the resulting conversations at the corporate table.

While the bulk of this book is focused on in-person communication, you will find a section on nonverbal communication designed to build trust, engagement, and audience attention, specifically in the context of distance-work videoconferences—which may, unfortunately, be the new normal for years to come. Interestingly, we may also need to consider whether AI will analyze our nonverbal communication and whether this is something we need to prepare for. The future may look very different from what we currently experience.

Accordingly, this book will walk you through the concrete process of eliminating any obstacle that inhibits your natural, strong communication. When you are able to work through your physiological responses to anxiety and shift your inner belief system about your communication skills, you will be able to verbalize your messages with strength and persuasion. The death of self-confidence equals the death of effective communication. However, self-awareness is the key to reviving and restoring your confidence. I know it will because I see it repeatedly with my clients.

Through the activities that fill the following pages, you will master the concrete scientific formula behind CQ. Mastering it will enable you to

- think quickly,
- structure your speech clearly and sensibly,
- craft persuasive language, and
- reduce the anxiety often triggered by speaking publicly or socially.

The book applies to many people on many journeys. Are you experiencing any of the following?

- Struggling with a presentation you have to give
- Feeling too reserved
- Dealing with the loss of a job
- Questioning yourself and whether you are heard
- At a crossroads with identity
- Not treated with respect at work
- At the top of your game and pushing yourself
- At the top of your game and not sure how you got there
- Dealing with change brought about by life-altering surgery or accident

- Maintaining confidence and internal dialogue during such times of pain and personal challenge
- Newly graduated and applying for a professional program
- Transitioning to a global from a regional role
- Trying to redefine who you are or get back to being "you" after putting your career on hold for parenting
- Regrouping after being a professional who was taken advantage of and made redundant
- Questioning your future competitiveness
- Being groomed for a future partnership or C-suite position
- Being overlooked for a corporate position you worked diligently to qualify for and left wondering why someone else was selected
- As a C-suite executive, implementing and managing change within an organization while motivating employees toward new objectives
- As a C-suite executive, establishing your personal branding and reputation as a thought leader in your industry

With dedication and the mindful practice of the skills outlined here, anyone—regardless of age, previous experiences, or predisposition—can gain the ability to speak with influence. You can. No matter which of the categories listed above is most relevant to your personal journey, you will find insights and interactive activities in the chapters ahead that apply to and will benefit you.

ABOUT ME

I affectionately call myself a recovering lawyer, but to sum it up, I'd say I'm a speakologist—I take my passion for persuasive speech that I developed as a litigator, combine it with the psychology and scientific research related to the physiology of nervousness and the neurochemistry of the audience, and help people from all walks of life master both as they improve their communication intelligence, or what my clients and I call "CQ." I support clients in unleashing their confidence through communication; this is achieved through a personal mastery of one's mind, body, and voice. In summary, I am a communications consultant.

I am committed to empowering people, which is what happens when you learn that you are in complete control of your physiology and you realize how closely linked your physiology is with your presence. Once you accept that you are on a journey of self-development, and that, through the science of communication and the very purposeful and easy-to-execute exercises in this book, you can track your progress, you become privy to experience your transformation as it unfolds through an intentional process.

When people are trying to learn how to speak with impact, they frequently pull bits and pieces from various sources. My goal is to make this book your one-stop resource to better understand yourself, address any temporary limitations and mindsets, and, using a holistic formula, achieve the transformation I believe is within your reach.

All I need from you is commitment. If I asked you to track your heart rate, protein intake, or number of bicep curls needed to reach your optimal physical health, you'd track them, wouldn't you? Isn't it just as important to reach your optimal level of communication? This is what I'm offering you—peak performance in any moment. Let's get started.

CHAPTER 1

What Is CQ, and Why Do You Need to Master It?

Knowing others is intelligence; knowing yourself is true wisdom.
Mastering others is strength; mastering yourself is true power.

—LAO TZU, FOUNDER OF TAOISM

Freezing rain slammed against the windowpanes of an Ivy League hall, the ice outside shimmering in the reflected light. Guests still trickled in, shaking the sleet off their coats and sliding into seats just as the room darkened and the stage lights went up.

After a moment, a man whose appearance suggested a retired professor approached the podium, adjusted the microphone, and said, "Welcome. It is my pleasure to introduce you to tonight's lecturer …"

The biography he gave was brief but powerful, and as the fortysomething speaker emerged from backstage, he shook hands with the master of ceremonies, smiled warmly at the audience, and reached into his inner coat pocket for his note cards. The young professor had become a world authority in his field in a very short time, and the results of his most recent research could have international impact. Those in the audience went silent and seemed to lean forward in anticipation.

"Good evening," he began, his voice confident and assured.

He proceeded to give a riveting lecture, barely glancing at his notes—speaking effortlessly. He made eye contact, it seemed, with each audience member. He was funny but authoritative. His words and his energy sparkled, and he finished to a standing ovation.

During the question-and-answer period that followed, he was calm yet engaged, answering questions thoughtfully. After the allotted time, he thanked the audience for their attention. Those in attendance were buzzing with excitement; they felt they had been in the presence of greatness and left feeling inspired.

It might surprise you to know that this renowned academic had once suffered from a debilitating fear of public speaking. When he first began to teach, he had used note cards as a crutch, staring intensely at them. He rushed through his lectures in hushed, timid tones, his words further muted by his inability to look up and into the eyes of his students.

Initially thrilled to have gotten into a course taught by such a young yet learned man, after just a few minutes of trying to listen, most of his students gave up, leaned back, and turned their attention elsewhere.

Although the professor had shared a great deal of information, he did not understand CQ—communication intelligence. The voice in his head whispered, "So much to share—where do I start? I cannot miss a statistic. Must make every point. Oh no, they're looking at me … now they're not looking at me."

His end-of-semester reviews were awful, despite his obvious expertise and careful preparation.

His department head met with him and told him in no uncertain terms that despite his brilliant research, publications, and reputation, his job was in jeopardy unless he could learn to connect with his students.

He knew he needed to do something. I was so fortunate to have crossed paths with him. He explained his goal. I am always thrilled when I meet someone so personally invested in lifelong learning and self-development—particularly when they are superbrilliant and as humble as he was. His goal was to become a riveting speaker, and he committed fully to the necessary work. This was a truly motivating goal for him, as he had originally become a professor because he hoped to connect with others and share his knowledge.

But his early life had led him to believe that brilliance was all he had. His parents, not knowing any better, had only been interested in his grades, not in him holistically as a person. So he had studied hard but had never learned how to connect with people. And of course, he felt anxiety, and it stopped him cold.

The physiological reaction of cold flashes—that head-to-toe wash of chill in response to heightened anxiety—is the body's way of cooling off the extra heat created as anxiety builds and the system kicks into "fight or flight" mode. It is this very natural human response, and it hinders the ability to communicate. You, like this scholar, need to understand the physiology of communication because it is a core component of CQ.

The professor and I worked together during the break between semesters. He turned his formidable intelligence and commitment to the task and worked diligently at turning his communication intelligence around. It was thrilling to see his confidence in himself grow.

The new semester began. The professor, a fantastic student himself, integrated all he learned. This time, he used the strategies he'd learned with me to work through his fears and beliefs about himself to connect with his students. And it worked! He turned his performance around completely, and his job was secured. He became one of the most popular professors at the university as well as a sought-after lecturer!

As I mentioned in the introduction, communication intelligence helps you achieve a psychological "state of flow" in daily communication and in those crucial exchanges that can change lives and careers. When you have mastered CQ, you will be able to control cortisol and the stress you may currently experience when communicating—regardless of where you are now. I've seen the results again and again—with CEOs of major companies, with executives who want to improve, and even with children who have been labeled "shy."

Perhaps you are wondering what we mean by CQ. You've probably heard of EQ, emotional intelligence. Well, our focus in this book, CQ, is the quality that will lead you to your goal of speaking in flow. You just need to commit to practicing the tools I have developed exclusively for this book. When you can speak in flow, you will have achieved the vocal image of your dreams, whether it is addressing a large audience as many of my international clients do or engaging in a one-on-one negotiation.

THREE JOURNEYS

Let's take a look at three different characters, each of whom is striving to master communication intelligence while remaining authentic to their true self.

THE NEW LEADER: GOAL TO CONNECT

A senior manager of a Big Four firm reclined in his leather office chair, reflecting on the past six months of his life. Last year, he had received word that he would be moving to a new office in England—a country both unfamiliar to him and very different from his home country in the Middle East. As excited as he was for the opportunity, he had mixed feelings about the move. Part of the reason for his relocation was the confidence his regional manager had in him to head up a new team, one that was being carefully chosen over several months to achieve a very specific goal. They came from diverse cultural backgrounds, each of them with different slang and idioms, and expectations that diverged significantly from those of his previous office.

Additionally, this man's title was changing. He would not just be managing his new team; he would be leading them. This was the opportunity of a lifetime, an opportunity that could propel the trajectory of his career. There was one problem, though. He knew deep down that although he was a technical guru, his skills would not be sufficient to lead this highly able team, who would be assessing his leadership style along with his every word.

The clock was ticking: he had seven weeks to his relocation. He had to make a perfect first impression. He had no idea how to achieve this. I was called upon to help him develop a CQ strategy, action plan, introductory speech, and messaging narratives. Before leaving for London, he committed to transforming his communication style and presence so he could make a positive impact during a first impression. Fortunately, the firm principals had made it their mission to empower future leaders with communication intelligence, which they recognized as a key twenty-first-century skill that would differentiate them and maximize their leadership capacity and effectiveness.

The leader had originally trained in it to improve his public speaking in the context of speeches and managing his team, but more recently, he'd been using it to extend his professional development, specifically in developing his personal messaging as he entered his new role. He knew that the first impression he made on day one of his new position would have long-term effects on the team's functioning and results, as well as how effective he was when viewed by his team. He was determined to purposefully craft his message and perfect it in the weeks leading up to his transition.

He'd made it his mission to improve his articulation, messaging, tone, and physicality of communication—all areas he'd identified as ones he needed to improve on. He still held the very first lesson of communication intelligence close to his heart: "Take advantage of every opportunity to practice your communication skills and develop your character so that when you are called upon, you can shine." This is a key message we share with all our clients.

Turning his attention to the near future, the senior manager began to think about the impression he wanted to make on his new team. How did he want to come across to them? What was the personal brand he wanted to portray—one that was authentic to him and that came across clearly from the very first introduction? His delivery would be vital. He needed to be certain about his tone and his message, as well as how he would define his leadership style to support his long-term vision and goals. He had little time on his side, and he had no idea where to start until he learned the formula we'll explore in chapters 8, 9, and 10 and the concept of vocal image.

As I worked with this man, he began reflecting on his communication skills in a structured and disciplined way. I was able to observe how he methodically considered which skills would impact the evolution of his career. He practiced articulation on a daily basis, consistently sending me videos of his practice sessions as a way of checking his progress. He was a stellar example of what it means to exhibit "communication grit," which is the engine that drives your journey to communication intelligence and, ultimately, flow. With effort and consistent practice, he remained mindful of his communication goals in his daily life and followed through on those goals with concrete action. He is one of those clients who will always remain in my mind for his determination and commitment—his grit.

Seven weeks later, this client of mine peered out the expansive window overlooking the River Thames. With Big Ben chiming in the background and crisp notepads laid out and ready, he welcomed his new team into the company's main boardroom. As they took their seats in the ergonomic black leather seats spaced evenly around the long table, he could feel them sizing him up—just as he was assessing each of them. Once again, he mentally ran through the message he'd been practicing nightly, hoping it was the right one to set the tone of his leadership and kick-start the journey toward maximizing his team's potential. He wanted to motivate and energize each team member in a way that would result in numbers, because that was how his performance would be judged. His vocal image had to reflect his leadership style.

He stood, all eyes on him, and instinctively ran through his pre-presentation routine, which he had been practicing for the past seven weeks. He had mastered this routine, which was compressed into the expanse of less than a breath. When he was finished, he delivered his message—masterfully, naturally, and with impact.

Whatever your challenge or doubts about yourself, you can do the same.

THE LAST-MINUTE SPEAKER: GOAL TO APPEAR FRESH AND VIBRANT

On a steamy afternoon, the regional vice president of an international biopharmaceutical company disembarked from her plane. In the past two weeks, she'd been in five countries and six different time zones. Her body was rebelling, and her mind was in a fog.

Once home, she hugged her husband and children, and then she sat down with her family, eager to hear about everything they'd done while she was gone. She had been subsisting on WhatsApp updates and photos of her star kids. Just at that moment, the phone rang. It was her multitasking assistant, who knew not to call her that night—unless it was urgent. She got up from the couch and went out to the hall.

"What is it?" she asked.

Her assistant wasted no time. "You've been called on to speak again."

"Now? Why?"

"They're asking you to speak on our regional corporate strategy regarding emerging infectious diseases, but"—she paused—"there's a wrinkle." The assistant said, "It has to be prepared in the next eight hours, vetted by our corporate communications department this evening, and then presented to ninety-two leaders in the international biotech industry … in two days. Oh, and it's in Hong Kong. You would have to leave tomorrow."

The regional vice president leaned against the hallway wall, processing the request while admiring family photos that hung in front of her.

"Ma'am?"

It was a lot to ask. The subject was one she'd spoken on hundreds of times, and thanks to her CQ training, she could speak at a moment's notice. But she was physically and mentally exhausted. Two days was not a lot of prep time to present at the same level as one who had time to rest and prepare.

"OK, let them know I've been informed and that I will have the presentation prepared as requested," she said. She commenced her CQ breath exercises to gain clarity of thought, then turned her mind back to enjoying her little ones in the time she had before she had to pack her bag.

By the time she arrived in Hong Kong, her message was refined and perfected, and she presented it with poise and presence. She then returned home and finally settled in for a well-deserved nap. As she cuddled her six-year-old daughter, lulling her to sleep, she reflected on how her CQ skill had become her superpower, enabling her to catapult her career forward and maximize her value within her organization while minimizing what would otherwise be lengthy preparation hours and stress in advance of short timelines and high-impact speaking engagements.

THE SELF-AWARE SPEAKER: GOAL TO STRIVE FOR PERFECTION

The Opera House is a masterpiece of contemporary design, a magnificent architectural representation of maritime legacy. In its short history, it had already featured internationally recognized performers from Plácido Domingo to the Baltic Sea Philharmonic, and this event was no less notable. Dignitaries from around the world were gathered to listen to a world authority speak on topics of global impact, and the master of ceremonies had worked tirelessly to ensure her speech was crafted with the perfect tone to unite the varied and distinguished audience.

Public speaking was nothing new to her. Over the past twenty-five years, she'd done it thousands of times. However, among the world-renowned audience was one particular head dignitary of the national government, sitting front row center, who had to be addressed perfectly. She had learned shortly before going on that there was a protocol for greeting him, a cultural ritual of sorts that she was not accustomed to. Although she was happy to adjust to the circumstances, the surfacing of an unexpected element—a detail she had not known to account for—was enough to set her stress response into motion and spike her cortisol. But now, it was time.

With grace and poise, she swept through the curtains and onto the brightly lit stage, hitting her mark and smiling at the applauding audience. Then, just as her CQ mastery taught her, she stepped outside herself.

As she stood on the stage, she could observe "herself" in the front row, watching her performing self—evaluating her breath, movement, glances, hand gestures, tone, inflection, body movement, and sway. Exactly eleven seconds into her opening remarks, she sensed her salivary glands beginning to seize, impacted by the autonomic stress response of dry mouth, and quickly flipped on her "speak switch," adjusting her breath and heart rate, and consciously lowering her stress response. The sensation of looming dry mouth receded, and she was able to proceed for the rest of the evening with a genuine sense of presence and the joy of addressing such a distinguished crowd. She had just experienced a communication flow state—precise, powerful, purposeful, and skillful—switched on instantaneously as required. CQ on demand—in action.

WHAT DO THESE STORIES TELL US?

I would like to invite you to think of three words that sum them up. Mind. Body. Voice. Everyone's communication intelligence journey is unique and purposeful, but our goals are the same—to be able to deliver a clear and engaging message to a group with or without time to prepare and to be able to instantaneously control our bodies in the moment, reducing stress and delivering a powerful, relatable message. You can absolutely do these things. All it takes is dedication to the mastery and understanding of the science of communication and language. Employing CQ can help immeasurably as you travel your own communications journey toward the point of eventual mastery. As you strive for mastery, add one more word to the mind-body-voice triplet: *connection*. That's right. Mind-body-voice-connection is the key to your goal of mastery.

We all have a right to be heard, to share our brilliance and knowledge without fear of judgment or worry about how our bodies will react in moments of stress. It is possible to control this, to align our bodies and minds and speak powerfully. In fact, communication intelligence isn't so much about better public speaking as it's about *impact speaking*—not merely speaking in front of others, but also speaking in a way that is memorable and impactful.

Self-awareness is vital to CQ—so much so that, when mastered, purposeful public speaking, be it for social, formal, or business purposes, becomes akin to an out-of-body experience, a state of flow, which is the ultimate goal for you as you complete this book. It elevates your self-awareness to the point where you can objectively observe yourself and the audience reacting to you in such a perfect state that you can modify what you are doing and adapt to those reactions in real time.

Essentially, to become a brilliant and impactful communicator, you must balance your worries about the words and shift your focus to who is receiving your message and how. You must develop an awareness of the psychology and neurochemistry of the audience. You must have confidence in your content knowledge and focus on sharing it in a way that has resounding impact, even in the face of quickly depleting attention spans.

Before we get into details, I would like to put this skill set into context so you can see what is happening globally as more organizations turn their "soft skill development" into a key success criterion in corporate performance reviews and an essential leadership develop-ment requirement. According to a Deloitte Access Economics report, "soft skill-intensive occupations will account for two-thirds of all jobs by 2030."[7] Communication intelligence is one of these soft skills. So are interpersonal skills, teamwork, creativity, and problem-solving, to name a few. Why are these soft skills essential? Studies find that employees with strong soft skills are more likely to thrive at work—and to remain in their jobs—leading to stronger businesses.[8]

Communication intelligence is my passion, and I believe it's crucial in our quest to "beat the bots." When I talk about CQ, I'm not talking about cultural intelligence, and I most definitely am not talking about technical and intelligence information derived from intercepting of foreign communications. I'm talking about mastery of communication skills, something I know is possible for you, regardless of what you may have believed to date.

Many people believe that you must be born a communicator, that these skills cannot be nurtured, and that a default switch within each of us is set to a certain skill level.

In fact, our communication skills are impacted by our emotions related to communicating. These emotions are often negative in nature, rooted in fear, caused by self-judgment, worry about impress-ing others, and often how our words may impact another's perception of our professional persona.

In light of this, I'm asking you to dispel that belief, to stop telling yourself that communication skills are innate. I want you to believe that you can learn these skills and that you can be trained to develop communication intelligence.

---

7   https://www2.deloitte.com/content/dam/Deloitte/au/Documents/Economics/
     deloitte-au-economics-deakin-soft-skills-business-success-170517.pdf.

8   https://www.shrm.org/hr-today/news/hr-magazine/summer2021/pages/why-soft-
     skills-are-important.aspx.

I have heard over and over from clients that while they appear completely at ease, inside they are trembling, whether it was the globally renowned investment banker who remarked, "Don't you just do it [e.g., public speaking or communication with strangers] over and over again for decades until it no longer bothers you?" or the management consultant who begrudgingly felt he was not partner material because he didn't have "it." It is time to flip our perspective and realize that this competency is within our control. It can be scientifically hacked—you can be hacked—and call on your CQ on demand.

We do not need to feel uncomfortable, lose prime opportunities, or experience missed impressions. While you may not have been able to access these skills over the past decades, there is no need for learned helplessness within us.

Your limited communication skills are not your fault. You have just not been trained on how to harness them. We are taught hard skills in school growing up—math, English, science, and languages—but sadly, few schools teach us how to master our voice, let alone our mind, body, and voice; this triangulated skill set of CQ is what I will share with you.

These skills, when mastered, allow you to communicate on demand, regardless of how you are feeling in the moment, regardless of who your audience is or what question is asked of you. It is the nurtured ability to be extemporaneous in your communication. For a few, it is a natural ability. For most, the mere thought elicits fear. The wonderful news is that it is liberating and is achievable by all if you commit and follow the steps outlined. You will literally "feel the powerful difference in your skill set" if you can achieve the ultimate state of communication flow through a four-step approach:

1. Suppressing brain activation structures associated with oneself

2. Dampening activation in brain structures associated with negative thoughts

3. Increasing activation in reward processing regions

4. Training four elements that influence the impact of your communication message:

   a. Your mind

   b. Your words

   c. Your body

   d. Your voice

ARE YOU SELF-AWARE?

As you make your way through this personal development journey, I will be inviting you to complete a number of exercises in the Tracking Journal that accompanies this book. These can also be completed online. I encourage you to use the online tracking journal so you can join our global community of CQ'ers who will have access to special content and updates!

The first question I ask when working with highly brilliant leaders is "Are you self-aware?" I am truly excited when I see hands go up, but I must say, more often than not, I could count on one hand out of a group of hundreds how many have started this self-awareness journey.

So as we start on this journey of communication intelligence together, I'll ask you the questions I ask them.

The first step toward speaking with communication intelligence is to take an honest look at ourselves and assess where we are.

ON A SCALE OF 1 TO 10, 10 BEING THE
HIGHEST AND 1 BEING "NOT AT ALL":

	How confident are you?
	How would you rate your public speaking skills?
	How would you rate them in the context of speaking with your friends?
	What about when you're speaking in front of strangers?
	Coworkers?
	Superiors?
	Do you really care about improving your public speaking skills? (If not, then there's absolutely no reason to read this book!)
	If you do have an inkling that you need to improve, where would you rate yourself now versus where you would like to be—aspirational number?
	How much effort are you willing to put in to achieve those results?
	Do you track your heart rate when in communication situations?

If you made it past the third question, welcome! You have the self-awareness necessary to move forward and master intelligent communication. Since you've made it this far, let's get into more detailed questions:

How would you describe your personality?

_____

_____

_____

_____

How would you describe your inner voice? Is it judging, critical, confident? What are the messages it sends to you?

_____

_____

_____

_____

Clearly define three of your personal goals for your communication skills development. For this purpose, a good goal is clearly defined and trackable, while a poor goal is too general and not easily tracked.

Examples of solid goals could include "to improve intonation, articulation, and mindfulness of my tendency to fidget when giving presentations at work" or "to be mindful of my tone and messaging during my next meeting with Person X, and to craft three messages I want to address the night before."

1. _____

2. _____

3. _____

The first step toward developing your communication intelligence is defining your vocal image. Let's explore this concept, which is fundamental.

KEY TAKEAWAYS

1. **Self-awareness.** Knowing others is intelligence; knowing yourself is true wisdom. The story of the academic turned riveting speaker illustrates the importance of self-awareness and personal development.
2. **Mastery is key.** Mastering others is strength; mastering yourself is true power. CQ gives the ability to connect with others, deliver under pressure, and achieve a state of communication flow.
3. **Communication intelligence.** This will help you to control physiological responses, connect with others, and speak powerfully, resulting in impactful and memorable communication.
4. **Create your flow.** By developing the mind, body, voice, and connection, you can achieve a state of communication flow, adapt to audience reactions, and deliver messages with resounding impact.

CHAPTER 2

Mastering CQ through Vocal Image Transformation

What is it about your voice that makes me want to hear you speak?

—ALLY CONDIE

VOCAL IMAGE

I would like you to reflect for a moment and ask yourself: When you look around your environment and view people whom you may or may not know, what characteristics do you observe to draw judgments about them? Do you label others based on what you observe? For example, if you see another in sportswear, you may label them as athletic; if you observe someone wearing glasses, they may be seen as academic. This is the more traditional concept of personal image that people are familiar with.

Now let's flip this toward yourself. I would like you to ask: How do you label yourself? Where did these labels come from? Did you ascribe them to yourself because of something your parents said to you as a child, a teenage encounter, or workplace messaging or interactions? The labeling theory[9] indicates that our identity and behaviors are determined or influenced by the terms that we or others use to describe ourselves.

Specifically in relation to your personality, please remember that, while your mind may believe it to be true, your label doesn't say, "I'm shy." It says where you work or who you are. It doesn't say your personality trait. We are a reflection of the labels we place on ourselves, according to labeling theory, and although "shy" is one of the most prevalent, it isn't the only one. When you label yourself as shy, you tend to become reclusive, like a crab in its shell. Whatever label you've attached to yourself, you are probably doing your best to act out. When you change your mindset, you are able to shift your inner voice.

In order to mindfully shift, you need to believe that who you are today is not necessarily who you can become. Not at all. Don't hide. Come out of your shell, and share the beauty of your mind through your voice.

I will ask you to consider a new concept to nurture called vocal image (VI)—that is, how you are viewed based on the way you communicate, the vocabulary you select, the vocal variety with which you deliver your messages, and the nonverbal messages you send to your audience. In addition, mastery of this concept requires an awareness of the need to speak with communication congruence—that is, in a manner in which your verbal and nonverbal communications match (and do not cancel out your message).

It is a rather abstract concept to be told to improve your vocal image, as it is a foreign concept for most. Having worked with thousands

---

9   Jennifer Delgado, "Labeling Theory: How Do the Labels We Use Change Our Reality?," Psychology Spot, July 16, 2019. https://psychology-spot.com/labeling-theory/.

of clients of all ages, I know this is not a concept that anyone turns their mind to until I bring it to their attention. What I invite you to open your mind to is that it is, in fact, like your thumbprint, unique. It can be your superpower, your personal branding strength, *if* you mindfully train yourself to understand the science behind it and pivot your vocal variety and language choice accordingly. I hope that from today forward, you embrace this concept and integrate it into your daily goal-setting vocabulary. I am asking you to take two preliminary steps in the process prior to actually working on your VI:

1. **Become aware of exactly what that image is.** Vocal image was traditionally believed to be solely focused on the impression that listeners form of you based on the sound of your voice. When I refer to vocal image in the context of CQ, I extend that definition to include the words you choose and their potential impact on the sensory cues of your audience.

2. **Learn the three factors that create a VI.**
    a. The speaker's physical vocal tools (the lungs, vocal cords, throat, mouth, ears, tongue, teeth, jaws, and lips) and the sound that is created by them.
    b. The sound production process and how we can easily fall into negative habits and inconsistent patterns if we're not focused on our personal physical voice mechanism and exercise a great deal of control over how our voice is used. Be aware of these areas:
        i. Intonation patterns like upspeak (i.e., ending a statement on a rising note, as if asking a question; it makes you sound unsure of yourself) versus downspeak.

ii.   Rate of speech, which may increase to, say, 162 to 175 words per minute, if you are nervous (we will show you later how to count words per minute).

iii.   Pitch: When nerves hit, you may speak in a higher pitch, due to increased tension of the muscles controlling your voice.

iv.   Finally, you need to be aware of sounding hoarse rather than clear.

3. The consistent, mindful usage of vocabulary that appropriately reflects

    a. how you want to be perceived professionally/personally,

    b. the message(s) you want to relay,

    c. the emotions you want to trigger from your audience,

    d. how you will adapt based on context, and

    e. how you would like to be remembered.

Note: No one factor alone is your VI. In fact, a combination of these impacts your efficacy as a speaker. And it doesn't take long for you to make an impression—people who listen to your voice for just six to twelve seconds make judgments regarding your looks, your intelligence, and more. They form an impression from the sound of your voice as well as how you use it.[10]

People often opt for a makeover of their appearance for the sake of personal or professional evolution. An ambitious intern may realize, for instance, that a more professional approach to wardrobe, hair and accessories could aid him or her in securing a desirable, permanent

---

10   L A McCoy, "The Power of Your Vocal Image," PubMed, 1996, https://pubmed.ncbi. nlm.nih.gov/8868166/.

company position. My belief is that, while this external makeover is crucial, what is everlasting is that first impression you make within the first ten seconds *verbally*. We view others through three lenses—trust, power, and ego—and we make quick judgments based on first impressions and heuristic cues.[11] In fact, based on the psychological principle of consistency, it is found that when people articulate an idea, they are less likely to change their minds, because they would first have to admit that they were initially *wrong*. Maintaining an erroneous notion, such as a first impression, actually causes less anxiety than admitting an error and adopting another position. You may have heard the old adage "It takes a few seconds to make a negative impression and a lifetime to overcome one." Humans instinctively judge others based on what they see, the words they hear, and the tone of voice that accompanies those words. Many do not think about the latter. My hope is that this book shines a light on how important the second two factors are.

In fact, a Harvard study found that "evaluating others requires processing complex information. Nevertheless, we can rapidly form an opinion of an individual during an initial encounter."[12] The study went on to find that responses in the brain were stronger when additional encounters with the social information were consistent than when they were not.

This is good news for some. While traditionally first impressions were notoriously persistent and would dominate regardless of how often they were contradicted by new experiences, recent research shows[13] that there may be hope to recode another's perception of

11   Heidi Grant Halvorson, "No One Understands You and What to Do About It," *Harvard Business Review Press*, April 14, 2015.

12   http://jasonmitchell.fas.harvard.edu/Papers/2009_Schiller_NatureNeuro.pdf.

13   https://psychcentral.com/news/2011/01/19/first-impressions-are-more-lasting-than-once-thought/22769.html?li_source=LI&li_medium=popular17.

you—but that is, of course, only if you are so fortunate as to have a second chance. Given that most do not have that second chance, let us focus on the need to develop our vocal image in a first impression.

So why get into all this research, you may ask? Simply, to share how beneficial it is to take control of and adjust your vocal image. Be impeccably groomed, and also be mindful of the messages you are communicating at all times—groom yourself and groom your messaging.

In many circumstances a purposeful amendment of vocal image can be useful if not necessary. For example, if you have labeled yourself as shy or introverted, the first step would be to explore whether the language you use in your conversations reflects qualities you may not be sharing fully due to your inclination to be more reserved. If you find yourself trying to adjust to a completely different circumstance in life, you may well need to adjust your vocal image.

Perhaps you are:

- A stay-at-home parent reentering the workforce
- A professional who is taking a hiatus from work to attend to care of the house and elderly parents
- Someone who has lost their job and must rediscover their confidence
- A person recently retired who must redefine their sense of self and purpose
- Someone who has been harassed at the workplace and feels their personal value is now undermined
- A person who feels uncertain about their future
- Someone who is preparing for a completely new role

In all of these situations, you must confront your identity as the primary source of it shifts. This is also frequently the case when military veterans reacclimatize to the civilian workforce. When you undergo a major life adjustment, more often than not, you experience an accompanying shift in communication needs. To be successful in the new context, you need to communicate in a way other than you were accustomed to in the past, but when you're unfamiliar with vocal image, such adjustments may seem nearly impossible to navigate. I invite you, as well, to consider that this is a golden opportunity to be constructive in your personal growth—to use this moment in your life as a project where you can apply the principles and frameworks in this book. Otherwise, we can sometimes "get stuck in our own heads." I invite you in those moments to believe that an intentional adjustment of your Vocal Image (VI) can be a fabulous growth opportunity.

Step 1 is to be very mindful of and intentional of which words you choose (or fail to choose). I will discuss this in detail below, but specifically in relation to your vocal image, I ask you to remember an important point: The words we think, speak, and believe have the power to open or close doors of opportunity and success for us. Our language affects our self-perception and impacts our future behaviors and attitudes. Here are a few "to-dos" that may help you in defining your personal vocal image:

SELF-LIMITING WORDS	EFFECT	ACTION WORDS	RATIONALE
Try	"*I'm trying to ...* " [lose weight, give up coffee, take on a new task, etc.] presupposes failure. It implies intention but with permission to fail. It deflects accountability.	I will	Instead, speak with words of intent and commitment.
It's too hard. I'm scared.	These two phrases damage your view of your abilities and your willingness to do whatever it takes to accomplish something.	Don't replace these phrases; banish them permanently!	Use words that build confidence. When faced with challenges, believe that you will surmount them and that you will learn valuable lessons from whatever the journey brings. This may appear to be challenging, but I can call upon my personal strength of {insert character strength such as resilience} to achieve x.
Can't	"*I can't ...* " creates a restriction on your success. It undermines your sense of power. It fosters a stronger desire to do the thing you can't do just because you're not allowed to do it [e.g., I can't take the time to go for a walk today; I'm too busy].	Can't yet Can achieve X if I empower myself with the following skills? May not be able to achieve X yet, but can with commitment including the following goals and milestones—be specific. Don't want to *I am unable at the moment. I do not currently have the personal bandwidth. I am on a journey to developing, as I have been unable to achieve that yet*	*Don't* is a choice. It's empowering. It reflects determination and willpower. Don't believe me?

SELF-LIMITING WORDS	EFFECT	ACTION WORDS	RATIONALE
Could have, would have, should have	These words are particularly insidious in their ability to impact thoughts, emotions, and behaviors. They imply a missed opportunity or a lapse in judgment. Their use can lead to feelings of regret and guilt, as they focus on past actions that cannot be changed, rather than on learning from experiences and moving forward.	I chose to do ** because, Next time I will	Shift language toward more constructive and forward-looking phrases (e.g., "Next time, I will" transforms a regretful statement into a plan for future improvement, fostering a growth mindset and proactive attitude).
A bit, a little	Leave these out. These phrases soften the expression of negative feelings. They may underplay your true feelings, limit the extent of your discomfort or disagreement, and/or inadvertently downplay the seriousness of the situation. They may also undermine the veracity of your statement.	Remove any qualifiers	Remove these words to ensure that the true extent of one's feelings is understood, to avoid underplaying significant issues (e.g., "That bothered me a little bit" vs. "That bothered me").
I think	This unnecessary preface to your opinion weakens your statement.	I believe, I have found, I assert, I firmly believe, I declare	Replace with stronger words (e.g., "I strongly propose" vs. "I kind of think that").
But	This is used to weaken what you just said.	And	Don't back off from your statement. Instead, add to it.
Have to Need to Must	These words sound dutiful, as if you are not choosing to do something but are being forced.	Want to My next step is … I'm eager to Committed to Envision Aspire to	Choose words that show your enthusiasm or that your movement on a journey to a goal.

Do not allow your language to steal your power. Rather, use it to empower yourself and manifest your priorities. The connection between language, words, emotions, and self can transform your reality. If your goal is to be resilient, confident, successful in achieving goals, and able to overcome obstacles, it is vital to know that the words and phrases you use shape your thoughts. Have you ever considered the language that makes up the beliefs in yourself?

You might be thinking that the easiest way to create a vocal image and master communication intelligence is to get out your pad and pen and craft the right message. That would make sense—if science hadn't already discovered something I'm going to share with you right now.

YOUR MESSAGE: THE LEAST IMPORTANT PART OF COMMUNICATION

"What?" you might exclaim, as many of my clients have. "I've spent all these years gaining the knowledge and experience I'm about to share, and you're telling me it's the least important part of communication?"

That's right—particularly in contexts that demand peak performance. Once you learn the science of communication, it makes sense that this is the case. An audience won't really hear your message fully until you learn how to deliver it. When people communicate, they tend to worry about *what to say* rather than how to say it, that is, on themselves as the speaker rather than on the audience; your personal power is unlocked if you flip this.

Focusing on "How am I perceived and why?" using objective critical analysis and concomitant preparation is what takes communication to the next level. I now invite you to shift your focus from you as the speaker to the person or people receiving your message—to the *audience*. For purposes of simplicity, I will refer to the receiver of the message as "the audience" through this book. I ask you to bear in mind, though, that the "audience" can range from the members around a boardroom table to your interviewer to a panel judging your partnership pitch to your team to your child, spouse, or partner—any fathomable context.

Communication, in and of itself, is simply an exchange of information. It's an ability that practically all living things possess. Simply exchanging information is absolutely fine in some contexts, but it's not sufficient when you are trying to make a positive impression. For that, you need to focus on your communication intelligence, which is a uniquely human skill. It relies on countless layers of paralinguistic prosody: those patterns of speech, intonation, and nonverbal cues that tell far more of the story than your actual words. Ninety-three percent of it, in fact. It also includes what many believe they do not possess, what I believe is a human superpower. That is, your power to control your nervousness in pressured, judgment-driven speaking contexts. We will look at each of these elements in turn below.

The common understanding of communication (one that is misinterpreted; we'll examine it in detail in chapter 5) is that it is composed of three general components: 7 percent is the content of the message, 38 percent paralinguistic prosody (sometimes called meta-language) and 55 percent body language, which we'll look at in much more depth shortly.[14] In other words, contrary to the intuitive belief held by most, our words are less than 10 percent of what other people "hear." I recall my days as a young, keen lawyer attending court. I was always prepared, organized, and well researched—the makings of strong "content" without doubt. To be very candid and open, I did

---

14   "Mehrabian's 7-38-55 Communication Model: It's More Than Words," The World of Work Project, July 26, 2021. https://worldofwork.io/2019/07/mehrabians-7-38-55-communication-model/.

not know then that that was merely 7 percent of my message. I had 93 percent of the delivery ahead of me. I had to compensate for my height limitation with my vocal image and presence. I had to ensure my tender age was not inhibiting my persuasive strength as compared to experienced, distinguished-looking senior opposing counsel, who had the benefit of years of reputation ahead of them. Back then, I had no idea that an eyebrow twitch, shift in tone, the almost imperceptible flushing of the skin, a slight flexing of a mouth muscle—all of these micro movements spoke volumes. I, like most young professionals, am focused on one thing—my message and my words.

Since childhood, I have been a curious geek, constantly asking "why" and needing to know and understand phenomena. While this surely drove my loving parents absolutely bananas, it is my happy place. In fact, I can obsess over ensuring I gain depth of knowledge prior to sharing my opinion on anything. This nature had served me well, especially being in a profession such as law, where I had taken an oath to protect and defend the rights and interests and neglect no one's interest in faithfully serving and representing the client. Having full knowledge and understanding is a huge responsibility, as your client is reliant on your guidance, and your reputation is tied to the advice you give. Needless to say, when I started down the path of understanding why some lawyers and leaders were more effective than others, I came to immerse myself in the science of communication.

COMMUNICATION MOVES IN TWO DIRECTIONS

I began to see more clearly that communication isn't unidirectional, from speaker to listener. Rather it also has a physiological effect on both. According to Dr. Kerstin Uväs-Moberg in *The Oxytocin Factor*, making eye contact releases oxytocin, the hormone that creates those warm feelings we feel when making a close connection.[15] For anyone who has had children, it is the bonding hormone that surges when you meet your beautiful newborn, related to familial bonding in animals, and it is tied to love and friendship in humans. For those who may not have children, it is known as the "cuddle hormone" or the "love hormone," because it is released when people snuggle up or bond socially. Species that have more of it tend to develop stronger bonds. It interacts with the dopamine reward system, which we will speak about more below. Put simply, communication has the power to engage the neurochemistry of the audience—it can literally be "brain candy" if you harness your ability to mindfully manage the three elements of your communication style. Alternately, it can destroy your presence if lacking.

Let's suppose you and I are speaking in person, and we make eye contact. That simple action causes our brains to release certain chemicals that make us feel more engaged and connected to the conversation. We physically impact each other when we speak, even though no touch is occurring.

That connection, where an intentional mind meets intentional body meets intentional language, is at the heart of impactful communication, and anyone, regardless of how we may label ourselves, can learn it. This means the experience is achievable by so-called introverts and extroverts, people of any age, and those with positive or negative communication experiences in their past.

For me, the formulation of a precise equation that would lead from communication intelligence to communication flow was a personal journey that began with the desire to know what I was truly capable of, who I could become. I wanted a scientific way of looking at my potential, and moreover, human potential.

---

15   https://www.scienceofpeople.com/mirroring/.

I know firsthand that when you're young, there's always someone taller, someone less shy and more articulate. At least that's how it seemed to me. In law school, I learned I could be successful by taking great notes and doing deep research. Researching communication from a scientific approach just made sense to me. *Why were some people such compelling speakers?* I asked myself. *Why were others, including better informed and more experienced speakers, less compelling? What made some able to verbally soar, while others sank?*

The concepts outlined in this book are ones I've tested not only on thousands of individuals, but also on myself. I have undergone a communication evolution based on the process I discuss here. In a sense, I was my own first client. From the time I was a prelaw student, I accepted and worked with who I am and developed a skill set accordingly; I was fully aware that I had cultural and gender programming that impacted how I communicated, what words I did or did not select, when I communicated or felt I would not be heard in a room, what tone or volume to use and how to gesticulate to overcome physical traits. I advocate this as the cornerstone of real transformation because time and again, I have observed firsthand that it works. I do not believe that, when it comes to communication, one can guide another to develop an authentic VI based simply on research and following "rules." At the heart of the method, I propose a mind-body-voice connection that requires self-awareness and connecting one's "final message product" to their Vocal Image. This method is based on personal experience and perspective and broken-down step by step to make it accessible for all. I would ask that you view each "skill" or "tool" as a piece of a puzzle. You may not initially see clearly how each tool connects with the other; let me assure you that once you put all these unique tools together, you will have completed your personal "Communication Intelligence Puzzle," and the result will be a transformed you and an impressively transformed Vocal Image and personal gravitas.

Before we launch into the science of communication skills, I thought it was important to share with you why I curated the "mind-body-voice" approach to mastering one's communication intelligence. You see, soft skills are funny in that they are difficult to measure in terms of progress. Unlike math, where you know if you have improved by the number of questions you get right, communication is not as easy. It made me wonder, as a CQ specialist, how could I be accountable to my clients and corporate HR teams?

As I've said, curiosity has graced (or some might say plagued) me since childhood. While I am low maintenance in all other aspects of my life, I overthink, and I do not do well simply accepting being told how to do something until I am confident I understand why it works or the rationale behind it. This translated into rigor when I researched as a student, invested time to understand my clients, and created a system that takes communication development to the next level.

I kept viewing lectures where people are simply told, "Do *x, y, z*," and you will be a better speaker. I knew through my self-awareness and personal experience that it is *not* as simple as taking the academic approach of structuring speeches, adding some persuasive vocabulary: "Imagine someone in their underwear," "Look to the back of the room," and "Practice, practice, practice." This presumes that all humans are the same and that the same tips work for everyone. What I have learned over the past decade is that our communication skills or perceived weaknesses are informed by so much more, ranging from childhood trauma to relationship issues to cultural restrictions and nuances to shifting mental states, to name only a few factors. Once we change our approach from learning "tips" to mastering one's communication intelligence through a personal journey, we open our minds to the intentional, self-driven development path laid out in this book. When we learn that language has a powerful impact on the brain of the audience, affecting our emotions, cognition, and social interactions, we are empowered. By using language intentionally and effectively, we can engage and inspire our audiences, influence their behaviors and attitudes, and create meaningful connections with them.

A lot of the guidance available at large is very general and does not get to the core of how to truly empower one to own their communication intelligence and create their own vocal signature. When I realized this, I sought to deepen my knowledge of the scientific components that comprise communication intelligence. I embarked upon exploring how positive-psychology-driven interventions can create *measurable transformation.* By using a set of tools, you will learn and applying them to recorded baseline speeches, you can view the progress before your eyes. It is the most rewarding feeling to have watched thousands of clients' eyes twinkle with pride as they see how they have transformed and proven to themselves that they can shine with their maximum potential. To be sent videos of speeches evidencing transformation, giddy messages reflecting how a client "flicked their CQ switch," clients sharing how others tell them "There's something different about them," not to mention post pitch calls recounting exactly which strategies were applied; the externally verified successes make me humbly feel that I have supported that person in their personal journey to transformation. So I invite you to get geeky with me for a short while so you can understand the "why" of how your body and mind impact your ability to be a super speaker. Let us learn how to master the mind and body physiologically and then layer the academic tools!

MAKE THE SWITCH

Once you understand the science of communication, its sub-elements, and how to perfect those skills—once you understand how every word you choose has the potential to make an impact on the neurology and psychology of your audience—then you can learn how to turn your communication intelligence on and off in the same way you would flip a light switch.

If you are an introvert who prefers quiet time and reading to interacting, learning this skill will not change you—nor should you want it to! What it means is that you have the ability to intelligently switch on your skills as needed based on the context, through physiological control, and then switch them back off when you're finished.

Thus, you have to learn how to step outside yourself and understand how to consciously monitor your heart rate, control your breathing, observe your physiology, lower your stress response, and self-correct. Once you achieve this level of self-monitoring, you will be best able to access your brilliance. Without self-monitoring, you can become lost in an unstructured fog.

So how do you start on your own journey toward CQ? Let's answer a baseline question:

WHAT ARE THREE SPEAKING OR COMMUNICATION SITUATIONS WHEN I GET NERVOUS?	WHEN I GET NERVOUS IN ONE OF THESE SITUATIONS, I THINK/SAY THE FOLLOWING TO MYSELF:	WHAT SHOULD I BE SAYING TO MYSELF INSTEAD?

DON'T BE AFRAID

Many know that public speaking is the most common form of social anxiety there is, and study upon study has pointed to this "condition" as having a severe dampening effect on many aspects of life and career.

I will be inviting you to shift your perspective, to stop looking at social anxiety as an illness that is out of your control, and instead see it as a condition that can be overcome and improved through daily intentional practice. Imagine how that could change your potential. Imagine how many doors could open that you previously assumed were closed. Imagine the collective global impact of people able to set their voices free and take action from the brilliance of their ideas.

Despite any genetic inclination toward social anxiety, despite cultural upbringing, despite any natural influences, such as where you went to school, what you were and were not taught, your personal insecurities or tragedies, you can be empowered to develop this skill set.

How rapidly you are able to do so often hinges on shifting your self-perception. Many feel that communication skill is limited by, impeded by, or linked to an intrinsic personality one often ascribes to oneself—and labels oneself. I hope you learn through this book that there are no limits to your communication development and that learning the science will only empower you to embrace and ignite what is within you.

Before moving forward, let us put our current mental state in context; let us remind ourselves of what is reality for the majority. We are taught so many skills throughout life—how to tie our shoes, ride a bike, write a research paper—however, most are never trained how to communicate, let alone how it is a critical skill that can be used strategically if one is eloquent and persuasive if we remember one simple fact. Communication is not about impressing and worrying about self-judgment nor asking yourself, "What if I forget what to say?" Communication is rather about *how* people listen to us and how their brains can best be impacted; how our message is remembered by the audience.

When you approach your communication skills development methodically, deconstruct your current state, become aware of your strengths and lesser strengths, you can then create a road map for personal transformation based on the scientifically grounded tools shared in this book. Once you can shift your approach away from fear toward courage and self-awareness, the focus moves from asking yourself, "What will I speak about?" to "What does this audience need from me to be inspired, informed, advanced?" This is step 1 to decreasing speech/communication anxiety.

Once we approach people as though we have communication intelligence that can be nurtured, we can move toward having a growth mindset on our journey to maximizing our potential.

We'll look at how in the next chapter.

KEY TAKEAWAYS

1. **Use the "mind-body-voice" approach.** Master communication intelligence by transforming the conventional "one-size-fits-all" advice into a unique journey of personal transformation.

2. **Develop your communication skills.** Effective communication stems not only from eloquence but also from understanding audience reception and impact.

3. **Use the switch.** Learn to activate your CQ like a switch, using physiological control and self-monitoring to adapt to different contexts. Effective management of social anxiety can be achieved through intentional practice.

CHAPTER 3

Positive Psychology and the CQ Mindset

It is your character, and your character alone, that
will make your life happy or unhappy. That is all that
really passes for destiny. And you choose it.

—CHARACTER IS DESTINY: INSPIRING STORIES EVERY YOUNG PERSON SHOULD KNOW
AND EVERY ADULT SHOULD REMEMBER, JOHN MCCAIN WITH MARK SALTER

I estimated close to five hundred people in the conference room during my keynote address that day, which made it interesting when I asked them to all stand up, grab their chairs, and place them in the back of the room so that they could stand together in the center of the hall. Accomplishing that took quite a few minutes, the chairs clattering against each other as the attendees shuffled around, murmuring apologies, until finally one large group stood in the middle of the floor, everyone looking at me expectantly.

"Lovely!" I said. "Now we're going to do some more shuffling. If you believe you are a strong communicator, go to the left side of the room. If you believe you are a poor communicator, go to the right."

Another two or three minutes later, the room was divided, somewhat more heavily on the "poor" communication side than the "strong."

"Perfect," I congratulated them. "Now, the last step. How many of you believe you were born this way, and how many of you believe that you can change?"

I directed the born-this-way believers to the left, and the ones who believed in change to the right.

Watching this flow from left to right, the waves of people rippling across the room, fascinated me. It never ceases to amaze me how many people believe they are born the kind of communicator they will always be.

I've done this exercise countless times with audiences, and inevitably someone asks the question that I could see on the face of a young man who was standing, looking uncertain and uncomfortable, in the middle of the room.

"Did you have a question?" I asked him.

"Yes." He paused and then said, "Can't you believe that you're born one way, but that you're also able to change?"

"Ah," I replied. "The answer to that question is exactly what we're going to speak to today."

I turned to the rest of the room.

"Whether you believe it or not, you have the ability to change, to develop a growth-oriented mindset. If you believe that you are born a certain way and are incapable of change, however, then you are less likely to seek out opportunities to shift your internal dialogue. And if you can't shift your internal dialogue, then you certainly aren't shifting your external behavior."

To have a growth mindset, you must understand that your abilities and intelligence can be developed. You must be open to being a "lifelong learner," which is a key success skill. You can become smarter. In fact, you have the ability to change the actual physical construct of your brain. All it takes is determination—and a lot of practice.

POSITIVE PSYCHOLOGY

But before we take an in-depth look at the concept of growth mindset, I want to introduce the discipline of positive psychology. It has gained a great deal of recognition and popularity—for good reason. It's a field that focuses on "the strengths that enable individuals and communities to thrive," and it is based, in large part, on the belief that people desire to "cultivate what is best within themselves." When this perspective is brought to bear on the field of communication, the result is a communication growth mindset, an understanding that we are not constrained by past communication experiences or so-called personality type, and that no one is born to a life of poor communication.

For an overview of foundational concepts that apply to CQ development, it is helpful to review the insights of four thought leaders in the field of positive psychology. They include the works of Seligman, Duckworth, Dweck, and Gawdat. We'll look at their work in further detail as you read on.

I promise you what I promise each of my clients: I do want to change your life, but I do not want to change who you are. Quite the contrary. Once you are a confident speaker, the real you will shine through.

Before we move into how to grow this mindset, let's take a look at the core of what we'll be building on—the five elements of happiness.

THE STORIES WE TELL OURSELVES

In Dr. Martin Seligman's book *Learned Optimism: How to Change Your Mind and Your Life*, the author discusses the attitude we use when speaking to ourselves (that little voice inside of your head that explains *to* you *about* you and about how the world works). That voice strongly influences both your view of the world and your behavior—because when you believe a certain way, you act a certain way.

When you talk to yourself, Seligman explains, your thoughts take on an "expository style." An optimistic expository style tends to view negative events as fleeting and specific to that instance, while a pessimistic style runs the opposite direction, leading you to believe that negative events are because of your personal failings, and the effects of those events are permanent and widespread.

Consequently, the more importance you place on feelings of helplessness and hopelessness, the more likely you are to develop worry, concern, or possibly even depression. Conversely, if you go too far in the direction of optimism, you could misjudge how much control you have over any given situation and see it, instead, through an overly positive lens.

"Most of us think we know what happiness is, but what are the actual elements that promote happiness within each of us?" asks Dr. Martin Seligman.[16]

His answering theory is known as the PERMA model:

---

16   Melissa Madeson, "The Perma Model: Your Scientific Theory of Happiness," Positive-Psychology.com, October 9, 2023, https://positivepsychology.com/perma-model/.

P: POSITIVE EMOTION

E: ENGAGEMENT

R: RELATIONSHIPS

M: MEANING

A: ACCOMPLISHMENTS

By building on these five elements, Seligman suggests, you will be more likely to lead a happier, more fulfilling, and meaningful life. And it starts with changing your mindset.

The key is balance—drawing on the pessimistic ability to realistically assess a situation while not letting that voice become predominant. Seligman refers to this as cultivating a style of flexible, rather than blind, optimism. I like to view it as being your own objective observer. Here is a cue to remember these steps with SAIMR: self-assess, improve, modify, repeat.

This has significant implications when applied to personal insecurity and self-perception. In fact, it means that you are in complete control of how you perceive and define yourself. This can have positive or negative consequences. When you consciously use a more optimistic expository style, you take better care of your health, believe more strongly in positive outcomes, and stand up for yourself more. You are less likely to let negative events overwhelm you, and you're even more inclined to have a stronger immune system.[17]

As Seligman's title suggests, it is in our power to learn optimism and train ourselves to break the cycle of negative thought—and that begins with self-awareness. In order to initiate this process, you need a mindful shift in the way you think and the way you talk to yourself.

---

17 "Optimism and Your Health," Harvard Health Publishing, May 1, 2008, https://www.health.harvard.edu/heart-health/optimism-and-your-health.

This in and of itself will not, however, achieve results when dealing with what is an actual fear for many. This "self-mind shift" is merely the starting point. It is an important and integral element of developing your CQ; without practicing it daily, your mind will not be open to the determination and skills development focus that will be called upon in this book.

The next essential element is to have a "goal-setting mind shift." This requires that you be extremely specific in every aspect of goal setting related to your communication goals if you are to be successful. If you have a goal that's too general or not adequately broken down into steps, you will abandon it as soon as your initial enthusiasm fizzles. On the other hand, when you're specific about the goal and track your progress toward it in writing, your likelihood of achieving it increases exponentially. Consistency and accountability are important components of reaching your goals and therefore of success in your journey toward mastering communication intelligence. Caroline Miller suggests these steps: Make a checklist of the steps needed to reach the goal. Add details to your list as you think of them. Finally, be sure to set deadlines. They should be specific, and they should be challenging.[18]

My clients often say I am hard-driving in my expectations of the specificity of communication goal setting, but once they have followed the process, they reap the rewards and experience the transformation, because it works. It is what you will see referred to below as "Communication Grit." It works because you as a person shift as a whole, as a person who mindfully focuses on intentionally developing your communication skill set. I will do my best to relay some of this gritty geekiness through the tracking exercises below in an effort to

---

18   Caroline Miller, *Getting Grit: The Evidence-Based Approach to Cultivating Passion, Perseverance, and Purpose* (Sounds True, 2017).

replicate what I am able to consistently achieve in person with my clients. It is essential, given my hope for each of you is not to shift but to transform. This will be your magic key.

GRIT: THE FUEL

Everything I've presented so far is linked by the element of grit. It is the fuel that will drive your journey to communication intelligence, and it will be key in your personal transformation.

The concept of being gritty is exemplified by the senior manager whose story I shared earlier. When you are gritty, you're not simply optimistic. You're dedicated in a way that involves setting specific goals, tracking your progress, keeping yourself accountable, recovering from setbacks, reassessing as you hit obstacles so you can find a better way, acting with consistency, and, perhaps most important, always keeping your goal in sight. Grit is what will move you from *working on* having a new mindset to *becoming* your new mindset. Grit is what will transform you from you to *you*—the *you* that shines brightly because you have internal mastery control of your being.

As we'll discuss in depth later, in *Grit: The Power of Passion and Perseverance*, Angela Duckworth describes grit as "the combination of perseverance and passion for long-term goals. It's not just working really hard and being resilient, it's doing all of that in service of something that you love that is interesting to you and that gives you a sense of purpose and meaning."[19]

Grit is essential to moving from a fixed mindset—one in which you believe a situation is as it is and cannot be changed, such as believing that you cannot speak in public and there's nothing you

---

19   https://www.google.com/search?hl=en&q=Angela+Duckworth&ibp=askj;ghXRXe
      mO%7CyobA8p.

can do about it—to a growth mindset. It takes daily affirmations, goal setting and reflections. Fueled by grit, a growth mindset doesn't believe in giving up. Instead, it shifts to believing, "Yes, I can improve, I know where I can improve, and I am going to be mindful about improving on a daily basis." I would like to take a moment and pause here to note, this may sound simplistic for some but is fear-inducing and insurmountable for the grand majority of the global population who feel helpless and captive to their beliefs.

Ultimately, the purpose of developing and practicing communication intelligence is not just to give a good presentation, hold an intelligent conversation, or have an impact on your team. Rather it's about shifting your *natural* ability and overall communication intelligence so that you are functioning at a higher baseline than when you started. As you will learn through this book, you can shift your baseline from an unaware, reactive one to one that is prepared, aware, controlled, and impactful—most importantly, self-regulated. You can achieve this by developing the grit necessary to make the daily commitment to intentionally practice your communication skills. The intense level of commitment is what makes you gritty. It is not about trying out a strategy you read about and applying it to a presentation. It is a moment-to-moment, scheduled, mindful, intentioned execution and application of the skills learned in this book, followed by self-reflection, follow-up, and tracked improvement.

You cannot assume that communication intelligence is intrinsic to all or a natural part of your development, that you acquire it in the same way you do your native tongue. You have to be mindful about it, practice it, unlearn what you believe, and reprogram your mindset.

The biggest hurdle most of us face in improving our ability to convey thoughts is the belief that we can't do anything about it. We feel out of control. We can have a deep understanding of our unique area of expertise, but we struggle to relate that knowledge to others, often experiencing a "delayed out-of-body assessment," which is when we say something and then instantly think, with a painful wince, "Oh, why did I say that?"

Once you have developed grit—and I hope some degree of excitement—to work through the daily exercises in this book, you will have the tools you need. When nervousness or anxiety set in, you will be able to stop, breathe, and set self-consciousness and the fear of judgment aside. You will be able to step outside your body and self-assess.

Think of yourself as someone learning the piano. First, you learn to play with your right hand, and then your left, and then with both hands. Along the way, you learn to read music, and you come to know certain songs by heart. When you combine these tools, and when you've had the opportunity to practice them, you can bring a sense of intonation, timing, and even voice to the songs at your fingertips. You eventually reach a level where you can play with your eyes closed, where you feel almost as though the music is flowing through you.

This is the same sort of natural flow you can hope to achieve with mastery of the tools that follow—a state of communication flow. Eventually, you will not simply internalize certain techniques for achieving the vocal image you want, but you will become able to modify your vocal image based on your audience. You will find you can remain mindful of your vocal image even as you monitor your audience—whether that's a single person or a crowd of three hundred—and their reaction to you. You will be able to ask yourself, "Is my vocal image off?" without panicking because you will have learned how to assess yourself as though you're on the outside looking in and to self-correct in the moment.

WHY AND HOW GROWTH MINDSET WORKS: YOUR BRAIN, YOUR MIND, YOUR MACHINE

Your brain has the ability to grow—to restructure gray matter in reaction to changes of stimuli.

Up until very recently, most experts believed that the brain was incapable of growth after a certain age, roughly around one's mid- to late twenties. However, in exploring the concept of neuroplasticity, we've learned that the brain continues to change throughout our lifetime.[20] As Thoreau so eloquently put it, the brain is impressible and adaptable, and new paths can be learned.

When you begin the journey of shifting your internal voice and any self-limiting beliefs, for instance, you're not just developing a new mindset—you're developing a new *mind*. You're actively focusing on changing what you think, say, or do, and as you change your default emotional state, your brain drops the old, nonfiring neural connections and creates new ones. For instance, a connection that perhaps once triggered the reaction of "can't" may now connect to a reaction of "can and will." Think of the negative voice in your head as an app running in the background of your phone, draining the battery. Just close the window and get rid of it.

As you learn to redefine who you are and how you want to be perceived, you actually rewire your brain to enforce your new way of thinking. In rewiring the brain, you recreate your internal voice, along with the internal image that drives your belief system and confidence. As this change takes place, you can feel a natural willingness to shift your behavior and develop your full potential, which is exactly *why* developing a growth mindset is essential and within reach.

---

20   https://doi.org/10.1016/j.stem.2018.03.015.

Also, a curious thing happens as we learn, no matter our age. The more we repeat an action in the process of learning, be it the trial and error of learning to juggle or the repetition of interpreting musical notes from the page to piano keys, the more electrical signals repeatedly fire down the same neural pathways, known as axons, from neuron to neuron.

As the repetition continues, the neural connections strengthen, eventually drawing the attention of glial cells that move in and protect the rapidly firing active connection, building an insulating shell, called a myelin sheath, around the active neural pathway. This sheath prevents the current from dispersing as it zips across synapses, allowing for a far more rapid connection along the neural pathway.[21]

Think of these stronger neural connections as the difference between taking a train, which chugs along and may stop several times before reaching its destination, and taking a direct flight.

This wrap also serves to reduce the amount of nerve fibers created in the brain. With quicker conduction, myelinated connections require less space and energy than unmyelinated ones. In fact, if nerves were not myelinated, the human spinal cord would be about as big as a large tree trunk.[22]

This is how juggling becomes natural—how, with practice, music eventually seems to flow from eye to fingertip without the struggle of identifying the note and where it falls on a seven-octave scale.

It's a skill to learn something through repetition, just as improving our intelligence and learning capacity is a skill requiring effort.

21   https://www.ncbi.nlm.nih.gov/books/NBK27954/.

22   https://www.ncbi.nlm.nih.gov/books/NBK27954/.

CHANGING YOUR MIND—LITERALLY

You have power over your mind—not outside events.
Realize this, and you will find strength.

—MARCUS AURELIUS, *MEDITATIONS*

Your mind is the one element that is entirely within your personal control. It is something only you can hear. It is something only you can direct. This is key in two respects:

1. Your mind is controlled by your inner voice, which impacts your vocal image.
2. Your mind controls your physiological responses to stressful situations.

The mind is symbiotically interrelated with three key indicators of success. First, it is connected to your mindset, which impacts your performance. If you can emulate a determined, adaptable, and stoic mindset, it will serve you well. Second, you need a defined personal communication plan, that is, a strategy on how to effectively cope with stressful situations. Finally, you need to follow through and execute the plan. Let's look at each of these communication success factors in turn.

It is my belief that simply reading that mindset can change is not enough to convince people. People often feel preprogrammed and born a certain way, with a limited communication skill set. It takes significant faith in a system and commitment to believe one can shift. If you have labeled yourself in this way, I hope that learning about growth mindset will shift your approach and give you confidence that you can master your CQ, that you are limitless.

Stanford professor Carol Dweck first observed growth mindset in action when studying students' reaction to failure. It was curious, she thought, that some students took failure as a temporary setback, while others were stopped in their tracks by it. Why the difference?

It came down to mindset. If the students believed that their intelligence was "fixed," then everything should come to them naturally. If they struggled with something, they felt dumb, and failure was the ultimate setback. Therefore, students with fixed mindsets tended to avoid trying things that they could fail at, out of fear that it would reveal a deficiency.

On the other hand, students with a "growth" mindset did not see failure as a setback. It just meant that they had to try harder, maybe approaching the problem from a different angle. The failure did not make them feel less intelligent. Rather, they understood that *effort* is the key ingredient of success.

Another important aspect of what Dweck and colleagues discovered is that growth mindset can be taught, and it can be taught *at any age*. It is called the *power of "yet,"* meaning that though you may not have mastered something yet, with time, effort, and learning strategies, you may well learn to do so.

Previously, most research focused on neuroplasticity of children. However, more recently, research has shown that neuroplasticity also applies to adults,[23] and we are more in control of our destiny and skills development than once believed. This finding is at the heart of positive psychology, and I believe it fundamentally applies to communication; I call this the Communication Growth Mindset.

---

23   https://doi.org/10.1016/j.stem.2018.03.015.

While it was mentioned above that we must turn our attention to the audience, I invite you to please pause for a moment and note that you are your greatest audience. The feedback loop in your mind, your "inner voice" is what can shackle you or set you free.

If you can shift your emotions surrounding your emotional response and triggers toward communication, this can be a very powerful step in your journey toward developing your communication intelligence. What does this look like practically? It means shifting your inner voice.

Look at the fixed mindset statements in the first column below. Do any of them sound like you? Try turning them around by saying— to yourself and aloud—the corresponding growth mindset statement in the second column. Sometimes all it takes is adding *yet*—the power of "yet"!

FIXED MINDSET STATEMENT	COMMUNICATION GROWTH MINDSET
I am not the communicator in my family.	I am not the communicator in my family yet!
I am shy.	I am not shy. I am uncomfortable speaking in this moment. I am not ready to speak yet.
I was born the quiet one in my family.	My current communication style has been impacted by events in my past. I will commit to daily practice to improve each element of my communication skill set. I am not bold yet.
I am nothing like ___; he is a natural speaker.	I am not a natural speaker like ___ yet!
I wish I could be the life of the party.	I'm not the life of the party yet, but I'm on my way!

FIXED MINDSET STATEMENT	COMMUNICATION GROWTH MINDSET
I wish I wasn't this quiet person who is never heard.	In the past, people didn't listen to me, but I'm learning to speak up and people are listening. I am not fully heard yet but shifting in my impact.
I don't know what is wrong with me.	There was never anything wrong with me!

Now choose two self-limiting labels like those in the chart above. Next, knowing that neither old labels nor past communication experiences need to dictate your future, alter those labels, as was done in the table above, to have a communication growth mindset:

_____

_____

_____

_____

_____

_____

I had the honor of working with a culturally diverse team of nearly 250 employees within a global consulting firm. These team members were each highly technical and top of class academically as evidenced through the stringent recruitment process, but a large number were limited in their leadership capacity due to their communication skills. This forward-thinking consulting firm had made communication skills a priority for their employees and prioritized soft skills as key to developing client trust and retention, especially in an era where AI was on the horizon to replace certain technical elements of the profession; the organizational focus was to groom its employees to maximize the human connection with clients, and nurture loyalty, confidence, and trust—authentically. Sounds easy, right? Not quite.

Through in-depth questionnaires of each employee, a key factor emerged regarding the cultural impact of being raised in certain countries where respect, authority, and tradition often guided what could/should/would be said to partners, managers, colleagues, and clients. It led me to wonder how I could create a program that would be equally effective to efficiently transform such a large group of people where there were so many differing cultural variables, as well as gender considerations. It was agreed that nurturing a team's "CQ Ethos" was at the heart of the talent development strategy. But how could I shift an entire team that was so diverse? One word came to mind—mindset.

Dweck's quest is to find out whether growth mindset and circuits primed by a growth mindset play a role in reopening and maintaining neural plasticity throughout life. In so doing, she said she "hopes to supplement the traditional view of a pure static intelligence that's sitting in the cortex with a much more dynamic intelligence that thrives on the growth mindset kind of motivation."[24]

When you have a growth mindset, you believe that you are not born incapable of certain tasks. Neuroplasticity makes it possible for you to physically grow your brain, create new connections, and learn how to do things you couldn't do before.

---

24   https://casbs.stanford.edu/news/
dweck-outlines-new-directions-mindset-research-sage-casbs-award-lecture.

It is possible to literally change our minds. Each one of us can learn to speak with impact and build our communication intelligence, regardless of how shy or reserved we are, or how much we may stumble over words in everyday conversation.

It starts with being open to the idea that you can grow and, from there, understanding how your brain and body work in times of stress. Once you understand this, you can see how it is possible to control your mental and physical state on demand.

If I can turn your mind back to the client example above, reflecting upon growth mindset theory, I believed this was the starting point to support the development of the consulting team above. I curated a bespoke program to shift the collective growth mindset by creating a five-pronged program that focused on the following:

1. Including self and audience in communication intelligence
2. Shifting mindset from a fixed to growth mindset using a series of activities and reflection exercises
3. Increasing knowledge base about neuroplasticity
4. Guiding on the importance of holistic development including both academic and physiological control/awareness
5. Offering a step-by-step system on how to track progress of soft skills in a measurable fashion through one's communication grit

We monitored team development over the course of a four-year project where attendees had to complete pre- and postattendance surveys and reflections. When we started with the CQ development program, there was a sense of fear, intrinsic labeling, limiting belief systems, and questioning of the ability to shift communication skills. These had to be (ideally) deleted or, at minimum, shifted in order to achieve sustained transformation.

It was amazing to see how employees transformed year-on-year. At each session, employees were told that it was their safe space to develop their personal communication competencies; that it was "their day" and that the firm was investing in each of them so they could shine as their best selves during their time at the firm and after. Through pre- and postattendee surveys, by setting clear intentions for each annual training program, and mindfully working toward specific goals, progress over the course of the project could be observed as assessed by video comparisons; increased levels of confidence, clarity in communicating with team members, and the ability to structure thoughts in a concise and persuasive manner were examples of what was observed across the group. It was so rewarding to hear the consistent reflections across attendees in how accessible the frameworks were in helping them improve their communication intelligence and how their increased levels of mind-body awareness empowered their leadership capacity. The collective mindset had shifted through individual empowerment. What was more satisfying was hearing CQ vocabulary—referencing VI, communication growth mindset, communication grit, amongst others—integrated into the partners' default language. The structured CQ strategy had been effected, and the CQ ethos had become natural and cultural. The organization had external measures that were a natural byproduct of the transformation—happy clients and increased revenue. CQ was not limited to work; rather, employees' CQ flowed toward happier personal and professional relationships. Maximizing CQ showed itself to be a win-win for all.

Moreover, the forward-thinking partners had unexpectedly set up their team for success during COVID-19, when employees were pre-powered to adapt their communication skills to the unfamiliar online environment. They noticed a significant difference between the employees who had had CQ training in the four years before

COVID-19 and those who had not. Their communication growth mindset carried them through the challenges.

Mindset is integral not only to your inner mind/voice and how you choose your language and communication style, but it impacts your leadership style as well. A *Harvard Business Review* article points out that leaders with growth mindsets are more likely to embrace new opportunities, make good use of discussion, and work out solutions with others to provide the best possible outcomes.[25]

Let us turn now to a key that will help us delete any preconceived notions about our communication intelligence: the impact of our inner voice on mindset.

POSITIVE PSYCHOLOGY AND THE CQ MINDSET—HAPPINESS IS A KEY INGREDIENT

Before we can go further, it is important to turn our minds to the concept of happiness. Why, one may ask, in a book about CQ do we need to discuss happiness? Simply said, very sadly, communication is the root of unhappiness for a large percentage of the global population. Historically, society has pathologized fear of public speaking, leaving people feeling hopeless about their skills development. My wish is that taking a positive psychology perspective will give you a new belief set that by using the strategies provided, you are in control of your CQ and that CQ is foundational to your happiness. Positive psychology theory applied to CQ urges us to stop viewing our communication skills gaps or lack not as an "illness" but rather an opportunity for wellness and happiness—as a means to thrive.

As discussed above, to build communication intelligence, you must first believe you're capable of such a growth mindset. This is an

---

25 https://hbr.org/2020/01/to-be-a-great-leader-you-need-the-right-mindset.

abstract concept to many, but you can take concrete steps to achieve this shift. One is to reflect upon your essential nature and consider what it means to be happy. The answer to this question will strongly influence your ability to have a growth mindset and/or to shift from having a fixed to a growth mindset. Let us deconstruct the concept of happiness and consider how it affects your ability to make this mindset shift. Two authorities have wonderful insight on how we can deepen our understanding of happiness. Mo Gawdat, former chief business officer of Google X and author of *Solve for Happy: Engineer Your Path to Joy*,[26] says to close your eyes and remember the last time you were unhappy. Maybe it was when your child threw a tantrum, or a client said a few choice words to you. Concentrate on how that made you feel.

Now stop thinking about it.

It's not quite as hard to do as it sounds. You can keep reading these words, for instance, or try the old "Don't think about elephants" trick until you can't help but think about them. In that moment—when you were reading this sentence or "not" thinking about elephants— did you feel upset? Probably not. You changed your thoughts, and in so doing, you changed how you felt.

Try this exercise by reflecting back on a time when you were fearful about speaking up in a meeting, negotiating a pay raise, running for office, or being at the boardroom table in a heated meeting.

Happiness occurs when life behaves the way we want it to. When it doesn't, we're unhappy. I know this is a simplistic way to look at it, but it's a very good starting point for becoming aware of what happiness means to us and how this impacts on mindset related to communication skills.

---

26   Mo Gawdat, *Solve for Happy: Engineer Your Path to Joy* (New York: Gallery Books, 2017).

Three relevant points of Gawdat's happiness equation are expressed as follows:

1. **Happiness = Perception - Expectations.** Gawdat argues that happiness can be increased by managing our perception of events and situations and by reducing unrealistic expectations.

2. **Illusion of thought.** Gawdat suggests that much of our unhappiness stems from the constant chatter of our thoughts and the stories we create in our minds. He argues that our thoughts are often distorted and biased, leading to negative emotions and perceptions. By recognizing the illusion of thought and becoming more mindful of our thinking patterns, we can reduce the impact of negative thoughts on our happiness.

3. **Intentional activities.** Engaging in intentional activities and behaviors can have a significant impact on happiness. These activities may include setting and achieving meaningful goals, finding flow in activities, and cultivating optimism.

Gawdat's *Solve for Happy* encourages readers to question their beliefs, challenge their thought patterns, and shift their focus toward inner happiness rather than external circumstances. By addressing the illusions that cloud our perception and adopting practical tools, Gawdat aims to guide individuals on a path toward lasting happiness and well-being.

Likewise, applied to CQ, when we view the development of our CQ, our personal happiness can be greatly impacted by our perception of events and situations. If we can master our mind, we can unlock the limitless potential within ourselves. You need to strive to become objective as to the root of your personal thoughts and which negative perceptions or historical events have created the personal narrative that plays in your head. Then it is within your power to make intentional steps on a daily basis to strive for communication flow and optimism—learned optimism as it is called by Martin Seligman.

ACCOMPLISHMENTS AS MOTIVATION

We all have a basic need to feel as though we've accomplished something. When we're rewarded arbitrarily, we lose motivation and, consequently, happiness.

"We found that even when good things occurred that weren't earned, like nickels coming out of slot machines, it did not increase people's well-being," says Dr. Seligman, referencing studies he conducted around the concept of learned helplessness. "It produced helplessness. People gave up and became passive."[27]

To avoid this kind of malaise, Dr. Seligman suggests the practice of setting realistic goals—ones we have to work to achieve but that are reachable. Happiness can be found in both the process and the accomplishment, he notes, as we can take pride in the measurable progress toward our goals and, when we finally reach them, enjoy the sense of fulfillment.

Bearing this framework in mind, I invite you to be very specific and pointed in your goal setting. To have a measured awareness and positive feedback loop wherein you are cognizant of your progress, you need specific goals that are set, achieved, and tracked. So let's do a quick exercise—your personal check-in with respect to your current communication skills.

---

27   https://www.nytimes.com/2011/05/17/science/17tierney.html.

SELF-ASSESSMENT CALLOUT

Ask yourself seven questions with respect to your level of happiness and how it is being impacted by your communication skills.

How do I rate my personal communication skills at present?	_/10
How do I rate my professional communication skills?	_/10
How do I rate my confidence level?	_/10
How much is my confidence level linked to my communication skills?	_/10
How much is my happiness level linked to my confidence level?	_/10
How much is my happiness level linked to my communication skills?	_/10
How much is my nervousness level linked to my communication skills?	_/10

Earlier I said that understanding happiness is the beginning of communication intelligence. This is true for two reasons. First, knowing what makes us unhappy, and why, is the first and most powerful step toward gaining greater self-awareness. Second, when we are unhappy, we are far less inclined to grow. Instead, we hibernate, burrowing into our safe, dark shelters and refusing to come out and take chances. When we are in a positive frame of mind, however, we are more likely to step out, take risks, and grow—to strive.

And when we're open to growth, we are more likely to commit and take tangible steps that will result in building greater CQ and achieving a growth mindset.

Once you develop a communication growth mindset and commit through your communication grit, the final piece of the mindset success puzzle is stoicism. Given that communication is something that pervades our daily lives, it is fraught with times that will challenge us and push us to question ourselves. Many more times we may fail to meet the mark we aspire to. In this challenge, however, also lies massive opportunity for growth, self-awareness, and self-development—if we maintain stoicism as our mindset. Stoicism is your key to not survive but thrive in times when you feel challenged. Stoicism mindset philosophy dates back to Zeno of Citium in approximately 300 BC; it was taught in Athens, furthered by Marcus Aurelius, and evolved to modern-day Stoicism, which is about achieving peace and resolve as a principle and core to your existence. Psychotherapist Donald Robertson treats anxiety using evidence-based approaches including cognitive behavioral therapy and Stoicism. Akin to your internal compass, Stoicism is "an art of living with happiness that aspires to be both rational and healthy." This action-oriented ancient philosophy continues to be of service, even in these times. Its practitioners rely on it to be more resilient, confident, and calm, needed qualities for any challenge you are confronted with. "Difficult situations are in the eye of the beholder," as I often say. How we approach them depends on how we perceive the *challenge*—we can either see it as a mountain of an obstacle and get turned back, or we can see it as a mountain of a challenge that requires activating our communication growth mindset. The Stoics searched for an opportunity for growth in every challenge. No matter what life threw at them, they had the choice: Would they be blocked by challenges, or would they fight through them? How can you be a Stoic speaker? John Dewey said, "We do not learn from experience ... We learn from reflecting on experience." This will be helpful in the exercises below. Adopt this mindset and grow!

REFLECTIONS:

Take a moment to record your personal intention to shift toward optimism in regard to your communication goal and/or personality style that is impacting your communication skills.

What my mind is currently telling me about my personality:

_____

_____

_____

What I want my mind to tell me about my personality at the end of this developmental journey; what shift I want to see happen:

_____

_____

_____

What my mind is currently telling me about my communication skills:

_____

_____

_____

What I want my mind to tell me about my communication skills at the end of this developmental journey; what shift I want to see happen:

_____

_____

_____

KEY TAKEAWAYS

1. **Harness the power of positive psychology.** Positive psychology focuses on building upon individuals' strengths to help them thrive. Communication skills are not static but can be developed over time. Our brain's neuroplasticity, its ability to adapt and change throughout our life, gives us the opportunity to enjoy lifelong learning and personal development.

2. **Use the PERMA model and optimistic self-talk.** Dr. Martin Seligman's PERMA model posits that happiness comes from Positive Emotion, Engagement, Relationships, Meaning, and Accomplishments. Furthermore, Seligman emphasizes the importance of optimistic self-talk or "expository style."

3. **Be gritty.** Being "gritty" involves setting specific goals, tracking progress, and maintaining consistency. It involves developing a "goal-setting mind shift" where goals related to improving communication skills are specific, broken down into manageable steps, and tracked rigorously. This approach is essential for personal transformation, moving from a fixed to a growth mindset, which believes in continuous improvement.

CHAPTER 4

The Science behind Vocal Image

To change ourselves effectively, we first had to change our perceptions.

—STEPHEN R. COVEY

Many of us are acutely aware of how we are perceived based upon the clothes we wear, the accessories we select, and even the technology we buy. When we think about "image" we tend to focus our attention upon the physical or visual impressions that we relay to those around us. This is the very traditional definition of *image*. Reflect for a moment and answer a question. Have you ever wondered how you are perceived based upon your language choice, the tone with which you speak, and/or the body language and nonverbal cues you display to those around you? Vocal image, first introduced in chapter 2, is exactly that; it is how you are perceived based upon the three main elements of your communication message, namely, your words, your tone, and your nonverbal communication. It is an excellent framework to guide your communication intelligence development because it requires you to consistently ask yourself three key questions:

- How do I want to be perceived by this audience?
- What message am I communicating to this audience?
- Is this how I want to be perceived by my audience?

When combined, physical image and vocal image contribute to our goal of establishing presence and gravitas; a judgment that is formed often within a few seconds. Clients often request a formula to "uplevel" their executive presence. Vocal image is a key component which is necessary to do so.

I recently had the pleasure of working with a client who is a country director at an international financial services organization. We had many strategic conversations about how her communication style could impact her progress within the organization. It is always fascinating for me to learn how factors such as cultural sensitivity, familial respect, work ethic, and drive can combine in so many permutations to create varied recipes for success. She explained her constant inner conflict of balancing how she was raised to be respectful, deferential, and culturally in tune with a work environment where others were vying for the same position and located elsewhere globally, and therefore not shackled by some of these "default switches" in their ability to pursue higher positions. She and many others around the world take pride in not asking to be promoted to higher positions, because executives believe that their worthy natures should be observed, acknowledged, remunerated, and promoted accordingly. This cultural upbringing, however, leaves executives in a conundrum; namely, how can one promote oneself while remaining true to an inner essence of humility? The answer to this was the framework of vocal image.

In supporting my client's future upward mobility within the organization, we used vocal image as a framework to language choice and a guiding system to direct her attention and awareness to the tone of both the verbal and nonverbal communication she used in all important messages, including annual reviews, mentorship sessions, television interviews, radio interviews, and even casual conversations with superiors. I shared with her, as I do with all my clients, that the vocal image you project to others is a reflection of your inner voice, which is the voice you hear more than any other, because it is the voice that speaks to you each moment of each day. If your inner voice has a lack of confidence and your language also reflects a lack of confidence, that becomes the vocal image that you project to the world. On the flip side, if your vocal image is carefully crafted in line with your ambitions, the language choice will likewise be pointed, driven, and action oriented.

I find people tend to downplay the importance of language choice and how words as short as three letters can radically change the trajectory of their success. Look back at the chart in chapter 2 on pages 42 and 43 and consider how often you use self-limiting words and phrases such as *I can't, a little bit,* and *I should have.*

Ninety-nine percent of my clients share that they have never considered paying any mindful attention to their vocal image.

Now, I'd like to invite you to conduct a self-awareness exercise to help you develop your VI.

DEEPENING OUR CONCEPT OF IMAGE: WHAT'S YOUR VOCAL IMAGE?

I have a big ask of you. I want you to expand your notion of the word *image.* I will take you through a four-step reflection activity as we explore the important concept of *vocal image,* which was introduced in chapter 2.

MY PERSONAL IMAGE

For this part of the activity and the next one, you will need two colored pens—blue and pink. There are some exercise templates for you to use in the tracking journal to complete these exercises.

LEVEL 1 SELF-ASSESSMENT

- Step 1: In blue ink, brainstorm ideas that come to mind when you think of what the phrase *personal image* means to you. For example, perhaps for you, it means being a persuasive speaker, being able to change people's minds and inspire them to action.
- Step 2: Also in blue ink, ask yourself the following questions, and write your reflections on "How do I view myself today? How would I describe my 'personal image'?"
- Step 3: In pink, write what you aspire your personal image to become; that is, your aspirational personal image.

MY "OBSERVABLE" PERSONAL IMAGE

LEVEL 2 SELF-ASSESSMENT

Review those items you just brainstormed and listed. Turn your mind outward to *how you believe you are perceived by others*. Take a few moments to reflect on whether how you are viewed by others matches with what personal image means to you. You can think back, for example, to your performance reviews, moments of conflict, or unsuccessful interviews, negotiations, pitches, or meetings, when the result was not aligned with your expectations. If you are unsure, you can ask your colleagues questions such as:

- How would you describe me as a person?
- How would you describe my presence?
- How would you describe my communication style?
- What are my communication strengths?
- What are my communication weaknesses?

LEVEL 3 SELF-ASSESSMENT

Using the blue pen, write labels people may assign *you* based on their impressions, for example, you're a reader, you're assertive/submissive, you have an accent, you're young, you are promotional/deferential/accommodating. You can also include adjectives describing your mental acumen, such as *wise, academic, intellectual, focused, smart*. And you can also assign labels based on your energy and temperament, like *calm, anxious, serious, lighthearted*. You might find that negative qualities make the list—*blunt, annoying, sarcastic*—along with descriptions broad enough to summarize your whole outlook: *positive, negative, hopeful, discouraged*.

In pink pen, identify words you would *like* others to assign to you—your personal image goals—those you strive others to think of when they think of you. Examples include *confident, assertive, determined, focused, articulate, organized, detail oriented, kind, thoughtful, accomplished, respectful, bold*, etc.

While the difference between Level 2 and 3 may not be obvious at first, the distinction is important. Level 2 is what the term means to you, both in general and in your aspirations for yourself. Level 3 is *your* personal image—your impression of the labels others assign to you and your goals.

We will soon delve into vocal image in much greater detail, specifically, how to define and achieve yours. For the purposes of this activity, review the above and reflect. Did you include anything about your voice, your confidence, how people view you based on the verbal (language, tone, etc.) and nonverbal communication you use? Even among those who've considered the factors we outlined for the first three levels, it's easy to leave out vocal image. Many people fail to realize how important their choice of language, tone, pace, projection, articulation, and similar factors are in how they're perceived by others.

Using your blue pen, write your current vocal image. Tune into your present way of speaking by any means possible. If you're not well acquainted with your own vocal image, there are a number of things you can do to start seeing it objectively:

- Ask for feedback from family, friends, and colleagues whom you know to be constructive and honest.
- Listen to your voice.
  - First, only audio. Listen to the quality of your voice. It sounds much different than what you are used to hearing, doesn't it?
  - Next, move to video. Watch a recording of yourself the next time you give a presentation. Study it afterward in the way football teams study game tapes to discover where they excelled and where they failed.
- If possible, review transcripts of your spoken words. While many components of vocal image—such as tone and pacing— can be best observed via recordings, reading a transcript may provide a better overview of your language choices. Looking at your speech in print can make things such as often repeated wording or "crutch phrases"—those phrases that don't serve the content of your speech but instead buy you a moment to transition to your next thought—stand out when you may otherwise miss them.

Using your pink pen, in the "My Aspirational VI" column, write your personal goals—what you want your vocal image to become. If you're an awkward speaker, you probably want to emanate confidence and security. If you know you come across as reserved, you probably want to be perceived as being in your element and energized as you stand at the podium. If you currently worry about seeming monotonous and boring, it makes sense that, instead, you want to engage your audience and present your material in a way that will excite them.

Filling out this part may be a breeze, especially if you are exceptionally self-aware. If you're having difficulty moving from the general thought that you'd like to improve and onto specifics, go back and consider the core features of a strong vocal image. Then branch out from each of these points.

Another approach you could take is considering the flip side of any present insecurities about your speaking style. If you're like many people, you have no problem picking out the faults in your vocal image. You may say that you're awkward, that you're too reserved, that you speak in a monotone, or even that you're boring. The good news is that these faults often unfold to reveal the very characteristics you would like to acquire and develop.

Are you having trouble with the above? In case you are feeling stuck on this new concept, here are some questions for you to reflect upon:

	MY VI TODAY	MY ASPIRATIONAL VI	GOAL SETTING TIMELINE OR OPPORTUNITIES TO PRACTICE
MY COMMUNICATION STRENGTHS			
MY COMMUNICATION WEAKNESSES			

I've walked countless participants through this activity. There was a purpose to taking you through the series of reflections—to help you isolate your perception of self versus how you are viewed by others. I hope this helped you reflect on how you may be impacted by your context or colleagues. Although I am always hopeful that someone will include vocal image, confident communication skills, or nonverbal communication skills in their initial reflection/assessment of their personal image, this is hardly ever the case. I am always amazed by how many people lack awareness of how—in terms of vocal image—they're perceived by others. I'm also amazed when people can tell me how much they weigh to the ounce and how tall they are to the quarter inch, but they do not know and have never considered the quality of their own voice. Those who haven't yet breached that level of awareness can't define what their ideal vocal image would even look like, let alone know how to modify it. For most people, even experienced speakers, this is uncharted territory.

> As you will learn, your personal image is inherently linked with your vocal image; congruence of these is key.

Right now, by simply going through this exercise, you are ahead of most everyone. Now that you know vocal image exists, you need to take charge of it.

TAKE CHARGE OF YOUR VOCAL IMAGE

People often focus on accessories to label an individual and assign an image to that person. With that said, know that you can control the label they give based on your vocal image.

So how do you want to be perceived by just that vocal image?

- Define what you want your vocal image to be.
- Create a set of goals to achieve and develop that vocal image.

Each one of the elements of a strong vocal image can lead to a number of related goals, based on your individual circumstances. For instance, let's look at the principle of speaking with authority. If this has historically been a problem for you, a related goal might be to consistently speak from your diaphragm.

Other pertinent goals could focus on monitoring your tone and articulation—listening to your own voice to determine its quality, whether it's high, low, or squeaky.

Another facet of speaking with authority is pacing. Ask yourself if you are pacing your important points and pausing appropriately. When you're under time pressure or you have butterflies in your stomach, you may be tempted to pick up the pace—but in doing so, you can inadvertently trample your own point. If you're rushing through what you need to say, and never giving your audience a quick breather to process what you've already said, it's unlikely they'll be able to really absorb your message.

Five qualities of a strong, confident visual image:

1. Persuasive
2. Structured
3. Appropriate in volume
4. Advanced, concise vocabulary[28]
5. Authoritative but adaptable to audience

Practice speaking with authority in the following ways:

1. Lower your voice by speaking from your diaphragm.
2. Monitor your tone.
3. Articulate.
4. Listen to your voice (plug ears with fingers): Is it squeaky? High-pitched? Deep and resonant?
5. Pace and pause (monitor whether your audience is receiving your message).
6. Be humble (no ego).
7. Be trusting.
8. Be sensible and clever.

When we're trying to learn what to do correctly, we can often learn from what someone does incorrectly. Eleanor Roosevelt said, "Learn from the mistakes of others. You can't live long enough to

---

28 Note that *advanced* and *concise* are related. Those with advanced vocabularies can typically express themselves concisely while still getting across the full impact of their message.

make them all yourself."[29] In fact, some studies suggest that we often learn better from the mistakes of others than we do from our own.[30]

Many people, preparing for a speech, focus chiefly on the content of their message—their wording: They assume that important content, worded well, is the biggest ingredient in audience engagement. When that is your perspective, you will, of course, spend the bulk of your preparation time and efforts compiling your data in just the right way, organizing your topics and subtopics so they transition smoothly from one to the next, writing down the exact phrasing you want to recall in the moment, and carefully crafting your conclusion. Most of the people with whom I work are technical experts in their professions. The greatest challenge generally lies with the delivery of content, not the content itself. As you will learn below, having a fine-tuned pre-presentation routine that addresses content and delivery will maximize the impact you make on your audience. While structure and wording choice of one's presentations and communication messages are critical, the greatest impact of one's message (over 90 percent) lies within the delivery, including vocal variety and nonverbal communication. As we touched on in chapter 1, and what specialists in the communication field have recognized, wording makes up a very small percentage of what constitutes effective communication. A speech of all words, in other words, is destined to fall flat.

The circumstance of the all-words speech becomes even weaker and less effective when you stop to consider how little time a speaker has to engage his or her modern audience. Many organizations struggle to communicate effectively with and develop engaging content for all

---

29   Legacy.com, "The Remarkable Eleanor Roosevelt," November 7, 2012, https://www.legacy.com/news/culture-and-history/the-remarkable-eleanor-roosevelt/.

30   Mark Brown, "Study Shows We Learn More from Others' Mistakes," WIRED, October 12, 2010, https://www.wired.co.uk/article/learn-from-mistakes.

groups in their multigenerational workforce—and it's especially hard when trying to engage with millennials.

Now that you have a grasp of what the framework of vocal image entails, let's break down its components to help you master your ability to apply this framework to your personal circumstances.

There is a duality to CQ! It's not just Self CQ; it's also Audience CQ and how you assess and influence it.

1. Self CQ: How to adapt yourself, your personal 7/38/55 skills, and your mindset.
2. Audience CQ: How to understand whether your audience is receptive and how to maximize their receptivity—specifically discuss neurochemistry of the audience, audience attention, recuing the audience's attention.

THE CHALLENGE OF DIGITAL DISTRACTION: KYC

We are going through an era of correction—many are intentionally trying to be more present, more centered, limit screen time, and structure device use. Many, however, are still what I view as victims to the "powerful psychoactive impact of the internet"[31] that results from the positive neurological pathways created when we compulsively check devices in this era of digital distraction. It is not anyone's fault … just a fact of life. Look down at a phone and each box has a red bubble with the number of new notifications appearing calling our attention—like Pavlov's dog—no dinging bells required, just a little red bubble with a number in it. This is our competition. Remember KYC: know your competition!

---

31   David Greenfield, "Digital Distraction: Internet and Smartphone Addiction," Psychology Today, 2017. https://www.psychologytoday.com/us/blog/virtual-addictions/201710/digital-distraction-internet-and-smartphone-addiction.

In this era of digital distraction, many in the audience, unfortunately, are eager to get to their devices, making it much harder for them to truly be present—and that's even when they're attending a presentation of their own volition because they're interested in the topic or the presenter.

Professor of cognitive neuroscience Torkel Klingberg, author of *The Overflowing Brain: Information Overload and the Limits of Working Memory*, quotes a survey of workplaces in the United States that found employees "were interrupted and distracted approximately every three minutes, and that people working on a computer had an average of eight windows open at one time."[32] Attention is the portal through which information flood reaches the brain, but brains lack boundless capacity.

How do you overcome the powerful lure of digital devices? By engaging. It's not enough to just offer compelling information. You must present that information in a way that makes your audience momentarily forget everything else.

We've previously discussed the concept of flow, developed by Csikszentmihalyi, and how it applies to communication. To recap, flow is a state of being in which you are fully engaged and fulfilled in what you're doing. In communication flow, you can lose track of time without your mind ever wandering. When audience members describe a speaker as "compelling," it's very likely that speaker was experiencing a state of flow.

Regardless of how brilliant you are, flow is the opposite of losing your audience because you're just a talking head. To the extent that you're remembered afterward, you likely will be credited as knowl-

---

32 Torkel Klingberg, *The Overflowing Brain: Information Overload and the Limits of Working Memory* (Oxford: Oxford University Press, 2008), 4.

edgeable. The threat is not being memorable enough to leave an impression at all.

If the audience leaves your event discussing the presentation rather than already tuning back to their devices and other distractions, you've made some kind of impression. But they may say, "He was really smart, but what he was talking about went right over my head," or "I just couldn't get into it." They may not even blame you—they may assume the problem lies with them. "Maybe if I was an expert the way she is, it would've been interesting to me." Regardless of who or what would bear the blame for a presentation gone sour, you don't want to get in that situation. No matter the subject, you want your audience to walk away reflecting on how much they gained from the experience.

As a leader and presenter, you're going to face situations in which your audience is eager to divert their attention to the next text message, social media post, or news update. You're also likely to encounter speaking scenarios where the topic at hand would traditionally be deemed dry or heavily academic or both—and it will fall to you to layer your message in a way that leaves your audience impressed with just how fascinating you made the subject matter. Know that you can do it. Chapter 7 will give you all the tools you need.

SELF-AWARENESS AND CONFIDENCE: THE CONNECTION

I've worked with people who've explained to me that they're normally loud and confident but at times can become shy and quiet. They may share that it's in these times of feeling shy when they lose their sense of control over their voice, that uncontrollable quiver that can overtake them and diminish their presence. With increased self-awareness comes the ability to pinpoint a specific problematic scenario, and often its solution as well. Someone who recognizes they lose volume and vocal confidence when they feel shy knows they need to finesse their tone by accounting for the psychosomatic variances they will encounter when something has triggered that shyness or fear of judgment. I am asking you in that moment of fear or worry of judgment to shift your mindset to one that removes the label "I am shy," or "I am (insert negative perception of yourself)" and allow your inner voice to say, "This feeling is a state that will pass." The move from labelling yourself to understanding that a situation is just one singular event is very powerful and essential to reaching your vocal image goals.

Another person may say, "In presentations, I'm quite loud and jolly. I feel that I come across as humorous, confident, and clear, but I'd like to sound more refined and mature."

A good example of someone who may have an easily defined goal related to vocal image is the business leader who knows they are perceived as awkward. This individual understands that while they may be seen as possessing a full suite of positive attributes—coworkers may find them nice, passionate, and curious—the perception of their awkwardness could interfere with their ability to successfully lead the team. This sort of individual will have had plenty to note about their vocal image in both blue and pink.

LAYERING

When you're working toward perfecting any speech, presentation, dialogue, social interaction, or other form of communication, it's important to layer the vocal image quality over your message. You can accomplish this by turning the powerful beam of mind-body awareness on your own physiology. This reinforces the earlier, critical point that successful communication begins with awareness.

As you work your way through each tool, bear in mind that you will layer tools upon each other with the goal of achieving communication flow and a transformed verbal image.

If you've always prepared for a big presentation or other communication milestone by focusing on content, you don't have to give that up. The content, your message, is still paramount. Your efforts are all about layering on the benefits of a planned vocal image to enhance your message.

COMMUNICATION CONGRUENCE

Before moving onward, it is important to note the importance of vocal image congruence with your physicality and language. If these are asynchronous, you will fail to make the impact you intend. For example, if you say you are excited to be speaking to an audience, but your tone is low energy and monotonous, and your body language is slouched, closed, unwelcoming, shifting, and otherwise distracting, you will lack communication congruence.

In the section on axons, we explored how the more we repeat an action in the process of learning, including the repetition of interpreting musical notes from the page to the piano keys, the more electrical signals repeatedly fire down the same neural pathway.

Developing your vocal image and communication congruence work in the same way. You can eventually gain such a hold on them that when it's time to speak, you will be able to tune out the once-anxious voice in your head and instead tune in to the present scenario, the present audience. If you think of that self-limiting inner voice as a series of apps running in the background of your phone and draining your battery—your potential—you can mindfully close them. In time, you can develop congruence and, eventually, communication flow.

THE GOAL

And that's what you are reaching for: the ability to modify your vocal image based on the audience before you. Whether it's three restless teenagers or three thousand executives, you'll be able to monitor how those listening to you are reacting to your presentation. As your self-awareness increases in tandem with your mastery of specific tools, you'll layer on your ideal vocal image so effectively that you'll find you can self-assess on the fly, and thus self-correct without stress.

To reach this point, however, it's important to take a look at exactly why vocal image works the way it does.

KEY TAKEAWAYS

1. **Vocal image control.** Perception of an individual often hinges on their vocal image. Self-awareness and a set of targeted goals can help shape this image, incorporating elements like tone, articulation, authority, and pacing. Recognizing and controlling emotional triggers, like shyness, can also help maintain a strong vocal presence.

2. **Overcoming digital distractions.** In an era marked by digital distractions, it is crucial for presenters to deliver information compellingly to hold their audience's attention. This requires an understanding of the impact of these distractions and strategies to create an engaging, memorable presentation, possibly using the state of "flow."

3. **Achieve communication congruence.** A speaker's vocal image needs to be congruent with their physicality and language for effective communication. Repetition and practice can help in achieving this congruence. The ultimate

goal is to adapt the vocal image according to the audience's reaction in real time, ensuring that the speaker's message is effectively communicated and absorbed.

CHAPTER 5

The Physiology of Voice

A voice is a human gift; it should be cherished and used, to utter fully human speech as possible. Powerlessness and silence go together.

—MARGARET ATWOOD

I catch myself wondering if, on average, when people think about public speaking—specifically, how one can be good at public speaking—they're simply focusing on volume control, that is, speaking up so those in the back row as well as those front and center can hear. That's like saying if your voice is loud enough, you can become an internationally known, sought-after speaker, traveling the globe and inspiring thousands. The truth is that so much is involved in public speaking, yet few recognize its complexity. My philosophy is that once you have a scientific awareness of how all the physiological, scientific, and mental elements connect, you are empowered to master your mind, body, and voice. If you aren't acquainted with the intricacies of physiology, and how your experiences interact with and alter it, of course you won't get the full picture of communication.

In the last chapter, you parsed vocal image to create personal goals when you picked up your blue and pink pens and focused on the word image as well as your beliefs and wishes regarding personal and vocal images. Now, we are going to glance behind the scenes to better understand the mechanics of vocal image. Once you have a grasp of this essential framework, you will be better able to follow the instructions and complete the exercises in upcoming chapters, all of which will help you achieve your vocal image goals.

Although the study of effective public speaking seems like a recent preoccupation, it was back in the second century AD that Julius Pollux, a noted scholar from Athens, took on the arduous task of determining all characteristics of the human voice as perceived by those on the listening end.

The account of his work that survived is not extensive, but the details we do have are telling. His lists include some negative qualities (such as feeble), along with traits that are noted as attributes of powerful speaking today: engaging, persuasive, melodious, and so on. Pollux equated the quality of melodiousness, in particular, with the impression of a sophisticated speaker.

Fast-forward to today, and researchers—while their methods and tools have certainly advanced—are still looking for answers to the question of what makes a person a powerful speaker. A company called Jobaline is credited with creating technology that predicts the impact a given speaker's voice will have on someone who's listening—and does so with 72 percent accuracy.[33] While Jobaline's stated purpose is helping streamline the recruitment process for hourly jobs wherein a

---

33 Rachel Heller Zaimont, "Can Your Voice Get You Hired? New Software Helps People Find Jobs by Analyzing the Sound of Their Speech," Fast Company, November 12, 2013, https://www.fastcompany.com/3038463/can-your-voice-get-you-hired-new-software-helps-people-find-jobs-by-analyz.

certain speaking style may make a huge difference, this type of study has exciting implications for our more global comprehension of speech.

In his book *How to Improve the Sound of Your Speaking Voice*, communications coach Preston Ni identifies four primary locations in the body where the voice can be "stationed": nasal passages, mouth, chest, and diaphragm.[34]

Ni describes a nasal voice as one with a "high pitched, almost whiny quality which can turn people off in a hurry." This brings to mind a common sitcom trope. Viewers know immediately upon tuning in that a character who speaks in a nasal voice will exhibit annoying personality traits and will likely rub other characters the wrong way.

Audiences do not respond well to high-pitched voices. If possible, you may consider learning how to lower that pitch.

While mouth voice represents a common style of speaking across many cultures, it's not associated with confidence, personal empowerment, or even having your message heard. The sound may be there, but the oomph is not.

Chest voice, another common choice, is pleasant and capable of sustaining listener interest. In fact, the only fault Ni attributes to this option is that "it is not the best possible voice."

That honor goes to diaphragm voice. Someone who regularly communicates via this voice "commands attention, 'sounds' more attractive socially, and is more likely to be perceived as a promotable leader," says Ni.

For clarity, there is nothing wrong with having a voice that is of a certain category; however, we must keep our eye on the prize, which is to connect with our audience by maximizing all elements of our

---

34   Preston C. Ni, *How to Improve the Sound of Your Speaking Voice*, Preston Ni, 2016, http://nipreston.com/new/project/how-to-improve-the-sound-of-your-speaking-voice/.

communication message, and this includes pitch. We are not looking to change your voice but, rather, turn on the appropriate pitch on demand as required based on your audience. This is a prime time to call upon your growth mindset—do not believe that your voice "is the way it is." Be confident in knowing that you can train it to resonate at an optimal pitch that is more engaging of your audience's attention. You just need the know-how. So let's go …

THE DIAPHRAGM: WHAT IT IS, WHERE IT IS, AND WHY YOU NEED TO KNOW

Projecting from the diaphragm is easy to learn. In my work helping people optimize their communication skills, I've witnessed clients make major improvements developing their vocal images with this change alone. So where's your diaphragm, and how can you make the most of it? First of all, know that the goal is to use air (breath) to increase the power of your voice. The diaphragm can help you do that.

This dome-shaped muscle separates your abdominal cavity from your thoracic cavity. To find it, here is a method I call the "cough test." Try placing two fingers on your upper stomach and then coughing. The spot where your stomach caves in is the place you want to draw your breath from. You can similarly find your diaphragm by, again, placing two fingers on your stomach. This time, though, purse your lips and force air out of your mouth as if you're blowing up a balloon. You'll notice a dent in your abdomen, and this is where your diaphragm is housed.

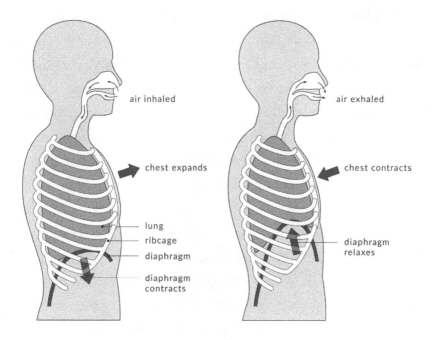

When you inhale, that dome muscle sinks down into the abdominal cavity, and when you exhale, it essentially bends upward. The goal is to locate it and then bring your breath from there. When you harness breath from the throat (mouth voice), you tend to sound high-pitched or squeaky and need to take breaths too often, potentially leading to a choppy way of speaking. Not only that, when you "rebreathe" too often, it negatively affects your memory and ability to hold long passages in mind.

Just through the simple act of locating the diaphragm and treating it as the new center of your breath, you can lower and deepen your voice so that you appear to speak with greater authority. This has additional positive implications for breath capacity and projection. The average speaker doesn't need to go as far as an opera singer—whose abdominal cavity palpably expands—but does need to feel and understand the power of breath, and how that includes one's ability to project and hold ideas.

We'll get into vocal exercises in chapter 9, but for now, looking at some of the basics can help you better understand the physiology of voice. In order to maximize your communication impact and ensure the audience can fully understand your message, you must remain mindful and articulate your syllables clearly. You must also remain in shape.

The social awareness that surrounds exercising our bodies and building muscle doesn't really extend to voice. This is a shame, because what's good for the major muscle groups is good for the voice—namely organized strength training. Any good physical trainer will extol the virtues of going through a workout in a particular order, perhaps recommending you work your hamstrings and then glutes, your abdomen and then your back. What they're keeping in mind this whole time is the necessity of alternating muscle groups so that each is subject to appropriate challenges and then given appropriate periods to rest.

Although you probably think about it in terms of these big muscle groups, you need to shine that same attention on your voice. When you train appropriately through regimens such as the one in chapter 9, you will set your vocal physiology on autopilot to articulate properly on demand. Just as you strength-train and plan your nutrition for optimal health, so can you plan your communication development by way of a daily tracking journal that will stay with you and, I hope, become part of your life long after you finish this book.

THE "RULE" OF 7-38-55

Much has been written about Albert Mehrabian, professor emeritus of psychology at UCLA, who conducted a generally misunderstood study[35] in 1967 that examined how people reacted when they heard words that did not match the tone of the speaker's voice. An example

---

35   https://worldofwork.io/2019/07/mehrabians-7-38-55-communication-model/.

would be saying, "I hate you," in a soft, sweet voice. In a second study, he compared a speaker's facial expressions with vocal elements, and found that, of the two, facial elements were more powerful.

Here's what he found:

- Seven percent of your transmitted meaning comes through what you say—your message—that content you've been memorizing and betting your future on.
- Thirty-eight percent is what the audience hears—the way you vocally deliver your message.
- Fifty-five percent is what the audience sees—your nonverbal communication.

Simplified, this rule provides a formula for how much message content, tone of voice, and body language count when it comes to whether we like the person who is trying to convey their message to a listener/audience.

From Mehrabian's work, we can take away the importance of knowing that when you communicate, whether to an individual or a group, you cannot depend on content alone. Although we'll use those 7-38-55 numbers for this book, they might, in reality, actually be 9-37-54 or another series of numbers. For our purposes, the exact numbers don't matter. What does is this: all the technical skills you need in order to be a good speaker are logged under content. Although that may not sound like much, when you learn to manage these skills and apply the tools related to controlling physiology, you can maximize that small percentage beyond belief.

I have mentioned previously that most people prepare for an important communication event by focusing on content, content, content. They believe it's the biggest piece of the proverbial pie. However, it's actually the smallest piece. Only when you've learned to prioritize the remaining 93 percent can you truly maximize your message. That's because your communication intelligence goal is never just to relay content. Your goal is to engage, to persuade, and to be memorable.

That "how you say it" 93 percent can be subdivided into 38 percent for such factors as articulation, elocution, and intonation, and 55 percent for all nonverbal communication, which you can visualize as follows.

7% CONTENT, STRUCTURE, VOCABULARY, PERSUASION ("WHAT YOU SAY")	38% VOCAL VARIETY, INTONATION, ARTICULATION, EMPHASIS, ENERGY, EMOTION ("HOW YOU SAY IT")	55% NONVERBAL COMMUNICATION ("HOW YOU SAY IT")

As we continue to progress through this book, you will learn science-based tools, and each one will fall into one of these columns. While it may seem daunting to view so many tools at a glance, you will surely feel prepared and organized as you learn these tools by category (content, vocalization, nonverbal communication). Follow along with the images as you progress through the book to help you track and remember visually which tool falls under which column! Track your progress as you move closer to your most powerful vocal image by making notes about each tool you can apply to maximize your skill set related to that communication message component. After you've put in time and practice with these tools, you'll find that you can easily apply them to numerous situations you encounter daily, including social contacts, networking situations, formal presentations, interviews, and even courtroom scenarios.

As you move through the book, I invite you to allocate each tool to one of these columns and create your personalized pre-presentation checklist. You can find a copy of this in your tracking journal.

CQ PRE-PRESENTATION CHECKLIST

This is a great time to pause and remember that whether you have a glimmer of a moment in which to make an impression, a few minutes in the form of an "elevator pitch," or the entirety of an evening, always turn your mind back to one key question: "What impression do I want to leave my audience with?" Remember that the human brain is primed to be in a protective mode, and it is constantly assessing people you interact with to determine where you fall on two important elements: namely whether you can be "trusted" (or are a threat) and whether you are credible and reliable in the information you are sharing (or to be questioned). As you will learn, humans are attuned to protect, so we need to keep this in mind when formulating "what we say and how we say it."

As much as you focus on how your audiences perceive you before you speak, can go into the practice of speaking, you need to address the elephant—or what may feel more like the crouching (cortisol) lion—in the room. That would be the fear within you, the fear that instigates a response within your body.

Let's take a look at that next.

KEY TAKEAWAYS

1. **Your vocal quality.** The quality of your voice greatly impacts the effectiveness of communication. A voice emanating from the diaphragm commands more attention, is considered more attractive socially, and is more likely to be perceived as a leader. Breathing from the diaphragm can lower and deepen the voice, enhancing authority perception and aiding in memory and speech fluency.

2. **Delivery is key.** Citing Mehrabian's rule of 7-38-55, only 7 percent of communication comes from the actual message, while 38 percent comes from vocal delivery and 55 percent from nonverbal cues. Understanding this helps refine communication skills beyond content, ensuring messages are engaging, persuasive, and memorable.

3. **Train your voice.** It's the key to effective communication. Specific exercises can strengthen vocal physiology, helping speakers articulate properly on demand, much like strength training supports physical health.

CHAPTER 6

Cortisol and Stress— How to Control Them

According to most studies, people's number one fear is public speaking. Number two is death. Death is number two. Does that sound right? This means to the average person, if you go to a funeral, you're better off in the casket than doing the eulogy.

—JERRY SEINFELD

Elizabeth, a nurse, was head of her class, extremely knowledgeable, and was approaching the final steps of accreditation. All she had to do was impress the interviewer. That was a problem, but one she could overcome. Although she could feel her heartbeat quicken and her palms grow clammy, she was determined that she wasn't going to let her anxiety prevent her from landing this opportunity for accreditation.

Then she walked into the office, her posture perfect, the smile pasted to her lips and saw past the receptionist to several people in the adjoining conference room.

Yes, the receptionist told her. This was where her interview would be taking place—a panel interview, that is. Elizabeth let those words register. Panel interview. A group of people studying her every move, watching and waiting for her to say something wrong. At once, she was awash in memories that stretched back to her early school days. She remembered how she stumbled over words when she was nervous and how stupid she felt when someone got an answer faster than she did.

Without another glance into the conference room, she turned and fled. That's right. She ran from the office, unable to face that panel she felt would tear her apart. She lost this major career opportunity—her dream career—even though she knew it was hinging on the interview. She was in her twenties when this happened. Now, thirty years later, it still plagues her, and she still physiologically reacts if called on in a meeting.

• • •

Joyce had been deferred for partnership at an international consulting firm. She was devastated. She had committed nearly a decade to this firm and shown through her leadership as a technical guru that she added great value to their team and the organization. How could they not have seen it? She had proven herself repeatedly. In her panel interview postmortem, she learned it was strictly a result of her performance in the moment. Partnership requires an elevated level of communication prowess that she did not showcase on the day she needed to. She was fortunate to have been given a second opportunity one year later. Was she successful, you may wonder. Could she overcome such a moment, do a 180, and earn acceptance into partnership? Follow her journey below and learn whether she managed a successful transformation.

• • •

Kaila walked into her interview as another candidate breezed by her toward the exit. As she turned to close the door, the elevator door slid shut on her fashionably dressed competition. "Breathe," she told herself. "You got this." Once the pleasantries passed, she sat in her interview and faced the dreaded question: "I see you left your previous job a year ago. What have you been doing since then?" She had prepared for this question repeatedly but, in that moment, her mind spiraled out of control, though she held her beautiful smile. In lightning fashion, Kaila started questioning who she was, whether they would think she wasn't worthy because she had taken time off to nurture her adorable baby girl, became angry that she was even being asked the question in this day and age, and wondered how she could compare to her competition. Would she be able to get her inner voice back on the rails?

• • •

Sara is qualified as a doctor. She made a decision to not practice because she committed to raising her five children. Rather, she committed herself to volunteering for charitable organizations. She was then approached for a paid position within an elite team that connected scientific, academic, and healthcare agencies to discover solutions to global health challenges and foster international scientific collaborations. She was approached for this position after completing a one-year volunteer position; clearly, she was selected for her proven abilities. Sara is a curious, perfectionist, methodical, research-driven woman who has a tendency to look for validation and questions her place at the boardroom table. She is aware that she overexplains, feeling the need to always evidence her statements with extensive research; but she cannot stop herself from doing so. This caused her to ramble and constantly feel unworthy while speaking among others. When introducing herself, she would always be questioned as to what type of doctor she was, and this would immediately feel like she was not worthy. She felt awkward when speaking in group meetings because her inner voice would send her into this loop and her mind would go blank.

• • •

In a workshop I led over 650 attendees. Each participant had to introduce themselves and tell a little about who they were. William, a member with an MBA, went through the motions with apparent ease, and then later after hearing others share their reflections of how they were fighting their physical anxiety throughout the exercise while discussing cortisol and stress, said, "It's not just me!" He went on to add that although he managed to hide his stress while introducing himself, he was panicking inside.

• • •

All five people I've just mentioned allowed fear of speaking to harm them in different ways. Elizabeth, the nurse, let the door close on a job that should have been hers. Joyce lost out on a partnership she had earned. Kaila's panic during a job interview allowed her self-limiting voices to take over her thinking. And William, the MBA, managed to hide his stress but still let it eat him up inside.

Sara probably could have overcome her nervousness with preparation and guidance and with less questioning of self. Nervousness isn't as difficult to overcome as the severe physiological reaction with which Elizabeth and William were struggling. These examples aren't fictional creations. They exist, and they pertain to what most of us deal with when it comes to public speaking.

For Elizabeth, William, and Sara, it came down to mindset, which impacted their confidence. If you were watching from above as these scenes played out like movies, you could see how early experiences emblazoned on our minds impact us later in life. The too-scared-to-speak child all too often becomes the panicked adult. The mother who sympathetically murmurs, "He's always tripping over his own words," or "She's so shy," is helping create an adult who will struggle to communicate his or her message because of a limiting mindset those words helped form. The teacher who sympathetically tells a struggling student, "Not everyone can be a good speaker," may be trying to make the student feel better but instead is putting a mental boulder in this future adult's path to success.

We will learn more below on how Kaila and Joyce applied their CQ to overcome their anxiety scenarios and mindset for success.

To move past the effects of such scenarios, we need to ask, what's going on here? Why is this reaction consistent across countries and cultures, in colleges and boardrooms? The common factor is stress, the common human condition. You already know that stress, including the types experienced by the people above, is dangerous to your health. You are probably also aware that we humans once needed the stress response to protect us from creatures bigger and more dangerous than we were. Now, however, that stress response doesn't know the difference between someone physically attacking you and someone handing you the microphone at an event.

WHY CAN'T YOU JUST CALM DOWN?

As humans, we are primed to survive any situations we view as threatening to our safety. But threatening, long ago, meant, perhaps, a life-or-death encounter with an animal we were hunting. Today's threatening situations, by contrast, are likely to be those in which we are judged and/or which have outcomes affecting our reputation, future financial situation, or well-being.

The explosion of all things virtual hasn't helped. Two decades ago, a calm state was probably easier to achieve than it is today. Recent studies show that social media and other modern-day factors exacerbate social isolation and feelings of being unworthy of love and belonging. As you'll hear me say throughout this book, the convenience of technology, including artificial intelligence, comes at a high price. In this case of public speaking, the feelings of isolation can bring on the fight-or-flight response.

ADRENALINE AND CORTISOL

Before we go any further, let's take a look at the chemistry behind the stress you may be feeling when you're expected to speak publicly or privately in a high-stakes situation, like the panel interview for Elizabeth the nurse or Joyce the consultant.

When your brain is triggered by what appears to be a threat, an emotional response occurs in the limbic system. That's where the amygdala, the center of emotion in the brain that affects your ability to think clearly when in this state, is located.

Then your hypothalamus, the part of the brain that controls body temperature, appetite, emotional responses, and more, goes into warning mode. Using hormonal and nerve signals, it lets your adrenal glands know you're in trouble. They, in turn, release hormones, including adrenaline and cortisol:

1. Adrenaline: All of a sudden, your heart rate shoots up, as does your blood pressure.
2. Cortisol: This steroid hormone steps in to make sure you survive the attack it's been signaled that you're experiencing. It

alters immune system responses and suppresses the digestive system, the reproductive system, and growth processes. This complex natural alarm system also communicates with the brain regions that control mood, motivation, and fear.[36]

What is fascinating is that, despite the internal autonomous response, the external presentation is unique for each individual. While one person may feel their legs go to jelly, another gets a lump in their throat, another goes flush red, another may feel the urge to flee a room, and so on; some may feel all of these together. The key is to control the internal response to limit what happens to you externally; this is achieved through mindset rewiring and physiological control.

Once you know that this is simply an "automatic" response your body is coded to execute, you can recode your personal "if then" algorithm.

Thankfully, there are some practical strategies to counteract this physiological response, which may also include nausea and having to fight for breath. You'll feel better if you change your thinking from I can't breathe and I'm going to collapse on this stage right now to a calm understanding of what's happening internally. Oh, that's just adrenaline and cortisol. I've got this. That same breath you're trying to control will help you take charge of those out-of-control reactions.

The good news is that once you no longer feel threatened, your adrenaline and cortisol levels will drop, and you'll feel your heart rate and blood pressure do the same. Then you'll feel a dopamine rush

---

36   Mayo Clinic, "Chronic Stress Puts Your Health at Risk," Mayo Clinic, July 8, 2021, https://www.mayoclinic.org/healthy-lifestyle/stress-management/in-depth/stress/art-20046037.

through your brain as you think, *I did it!* Furthermore, you might have serotonin, which produces the feeling of being respected by other people, in the mix. People in the audience might applaud. You look out at them and see smiles and nods. Oxytocin creates the feeling of safety with others, and you may well experience that too. No more fight or flight. However, if you've just started to address an audience or an interview panel holding your future in its hands, you can't wait for that stress to pass. You have to deal with it immediately—in the moment.

The Problem: Stress

The Solution: Awareness

The Success: Training your mind-body-voice connection

TRAINING THE VAGUS NERVE

After working with thousands of individuals, I have noticed a consistent trend of how people are programmed to believe "they are who they are and react as they do" in stressful situations. The one element which I find fascinating is the humility with which people approach their personal development after they learn that they can stimulate their vagus nerve—their superpower.

The vagus nerve, also known as the tenth cranial nerve, is a long nerve that runs from the brain stem down to the abdomen and is involved in a variety of bodily functions, including digestion, heart rate, and breathing. It is also involved in the body's stress response and can play a role in regulating anxiety levels.

When we experience anxiety or stress, the sympathetic nervous system, which is responsible for the body's fight-or-flight response, becomes activated. This can cause a number of physical symptoms, including increased heart rate, sweating, and trembling. However, the vagus nerve can help to counteract these symptoms by activating the parasympathetic nervous system, which is responsible for calming the body down.

One of the ways that the vagus nerve can activate the parasympathetic nervous system is through a process called "vagal tone." Vagal tone refers to the degree to which the vagus nerve is able to regulate the body's stress response. People with high vagal tone are generally able to calm themselves down more quickly after a stressful event, while those with low vagal tone may struggle to regulate their stress levels.

Research has shown that individuals with high levels of public speaking anxiety may have lower vagal tone than those who do not experience such anxiety. This suggests that the vagus nerve may play a role in regulating anxiety levels during public speaking, and that improving vagal tone may be a useful strategy for reducing public speaking anxiety. Techniques such as deep breathing, meditation, and yoga have been shown to increase vagal tone and may be helpful for individuals who struggle with public speaking anxiety.

You may not know it, but you have the ability to hack your hormones. Once you master this, you multiply your potential exponentially. Overtime, you can switch between stressed/relaxed states—switch them on and off—physically in full control of your physiology.

Step 1 is to bring awareness to what your body does in a stressful situation.

- While standing, place index finger and middle fingers together to find your pulse on neck. (I would ask that you do not use a smart watch for this. Rather bring awareness to your body and feel your pulse, your heart rate and how your body feels in the moment.)
- Put timer on for fifteen seconds.
- Count the number of pulses in fifteen seconds and multiply by four. This is your Baseline BPM (beats per minute) in a nonstressful situation.
- With the timer on, do squats for sixty seconds.
- Count the number of squats in sixty seconds.
- With the timer on, for fifteen seconds, count pulse using your fingers and multiplying by four. This is your stressed state BPM in stressful situation. Bring awareness to any sensations in your body and record them.

Your target will be to have your stressed BPM match your relaxed state BPM in stressful situations. The strategies below will help you achieve this override of your stressed state BPM.

Step 2 is to build an understanding of what the human body does and then nurture a mindful awareness of how your unique body operates in these situations. After periods of anxiety and stress, you need to bring your body back to that calm state of homeostasis. A key to doing so is to strive to achieve a state called "healthy vagal tone," which entails emotional regulation, greater connection, and better physical health by overriding your fight-or-flight response. Think of it as your success switch in stressful moments.

The vagus nerve (one of twelve pairs of cranial nerves within the sensory-somatic nervous system and parasympathetic nervous system) is responsible for that. Originating at the brain stem in the medulla oblongata, the tenth pair of cranial nerves travel down the sides of your neck, across your chest, and down through your abdomen. So named because it wanders like a vagabond, sending out sensory fibers from your brain stem to your visceral organs, the vagus nerve is the longest of the cranial nerves.[37]

This nerve is the sensory network alerting your brain to what's happening in your stomach, intestines, lungs and heart, spleen, liver, and kidneys, as well as numerous other nerves that are involved in everything from talking to eye contact to facial expressions to your ability to tune in to other people's voices. Made up of thousands upon thousands of fibers, it operates far below the level of your conscious mind and plays a vital role in sustaining your overall wellness.

Equally important, it is an essential part of the parasympathetic nervous system, which is responsible for calming organs after the stressed fight-or-flight adrenaline response to danger.[38]

The stronger the vagus activity, the quicker your body can recover from stress and the stronger your body will be at regulating blood glucose levels. On the other hand, the vagus nerve can't differentiate between the stress and insecurity you feel before a speech and legitimate physical danger. So there you are with a dry mouth, a

---

37   Jordan Rosenfeld, "9 Fascinating Facts about the Vagus Nerve," Mental Floss, November 13, 2018, http://mentalfloss.com/ article/65710/9-nervy-facts-about-vagus-nerve.

38   MELT, "Vagus Nerve: The Nerve You Need to Know About," MELT (blog), April 2, 2021, https://www.meltmethod.com/blog/vagus-nerve/.

quaking stomach, sweaty palms, and a voice that sounds stretched thin—because it is. However, you can learn how to use the vagus nerve to help ease anxiety.

An electrocardiogram can determine vagal tone. MELT (Myofascial Energetic Length Technique) creator Sue Hitzmann says you can improve vagal tone in the following ways:

- Taking a cold shower. Or, for the faint of heart, putting your face in ice water for twenty seconds and then repeating five to ten times.
- Singing, laughing, hugging, all of which release those stress-reducing hormones, oxytocin, and serotonin.
- Keeping your gut healthy. Hitzmann says that intermittent fasting or reducing calories has been shown to increase the high-frequency heart-rate variability, which is a marker of vagal tone.
- Altering heart-rate variability.
- Reducing jaw tension. Misalignment of the jaw can cause low vagal tone.[39]

Here is a massage technique to stimulate the vagus nerve and quickly regulate your nervous system—you may feel some change in breathing or sigh or yawn:

1. Place your index finger on the pressure point at the back of your ear and massage gently for thirty seconds.
2. Massage gently in a circular motion at the top of your outer ear for thirty seconds.

(There are others, which are harder to explain in book format.)

Tapping, or Emotional Freedom Techniques (EFT), is a self-help method that combines cognitive therapy and acupressure. It involves

---

39   MELT, "Vagus Nerve."

tapping specific points on the body while focusing on negative emotions or sensations, which can help reduce stress and anxiety. This process works by lowering cortisol levels, the body's stress hormone, and soothing the nervous system, shifting it from a "fight-or-flight" response to a more relaxed state. This technique helps center the mind, breaking the cycle of repetitive anxious thoughts and promoting present-moment awareness.

The act of tapping and verbally acknowledging emotional issues aids in processing these emotions in a controlled manner, reducing their intensity. It also increases blood flow, alleviating physical stress symptoms like muscle tension and headaches. This can empower you with a tool for managing your emotions while enhancing body awareness, allowing for your early recognition and intervention of stress and anxiety.

This technique is convenient and accessible, requiring no special equipment, and can be done anywhere at any time, especially right before a presentation or meeting in a private space.

A clinically proven way to stimulate your vagus nerve involves stimulation with an implanted device. However, endurance athlete and coach Christopher Bergland's "Vagus Nerve Survival Guide" suggests a number of techniques, including practicing breathing from the diaphragm, getting exercise daily, meeting with others in person, being honest with oneself, and helping other people.[40]

Activities like yoga have also proven helpful because the guided breathing exercises calm your heart rate and lower your blood pressure. In one study, slow breathing exercises improved autonomic functions in healthy participants. Fast breathing did not. Fast breathing makes

---

40 Christopher Bergland, "A Vagus Nerve Survival Guide to Combat Fight-or-Flight Urges," Psychology Today, May 15, 2017, https://www.psychologytoday.com/us/blog/the-athletes-way/201705/vagus-nerve-survival-guide-combat-fight-or-flight-urges.

your body think you're running from predators, and you know what happens then—a stress response.[41]

When you turn your mind to this, it can be the trigger to you being kind to yourself as you realize it is the first step in your journey to master yourself.

HORMONAL SHIFTS

Remember that many factors can influence your cortisol and your ability to control your anxiety. For example, as one ages and hormones shift, one might find it more challenging to regulate one's physiological responses in anxiety-provoking situations. As explained so beautifully by Dr. Mindy Pelz, a loss of certain hormones in women post-forty such as progesterone, which stimulates GABA (gamma-aminobutyric acid) which calms us and keeps the nervous system in a relaxed state, may lead to a less controlled response. This can have a significant impact in situations where we feel challenged including negotiations, board meetings, high-stakes presentations or even personal contexts.

Lower levels of progesterone and GABA have a profound impact on stress management. Progesterone, a hormone with calming effects on the brain, when reduced, lessens our ability to mitigate stress and anxiety. This decline directly influences cortisol regulation, leading to possible chronic elevation of this stress hormone. GABA, the brain's primary inhibitory neurotransmitter, acts as a neurological "brake." Lowered GABA levels mean this brake is less effective, resulting in heightened neural activity and increased stress sensitivity. This imbalance disrupts the cortisol feedback loop, prolonging stress responses and complicating emotional regulation. The net result is an individual more prone to

---

41   Dave Asprey, "How to Strengthen Your Vagus Nerve to Upgrade Your Whole Body," accessed November 10, 2021, https://daveasprey.com/vagus-nerve-vagal-response/.

stress, with increased anxiety and mood fluctuations. Physical realities such as this should be kept in mind when considering our strategies and self-awareness in speaking contexts. Practicing this potpourri of exercises can help train your mind and brain to override your body on demand.

BREATH TECHNIQUES

Breathing can give you away—anxiety and all. If you are trying to mask your facial emotions, the way you breathe will still reveal what's going on. Shallow breaths signal frustration. An occasional deep breath signals the speaker's need to pull in a large amount of oxygen to calm their nerves. Cortisol is the culprit, and you can deal with it. There are a multitude of breath exercises one can practice to train one's body to decrease its cortisol response. Think of this as a box of chocolates with different flavors—try a new one each day!

BOX BREATHING

In chapter 7, we're going to look at a prompt to help you remember how to breathe to reduce cortisol, even while you're making a presentation. But before we get to that, here's an introduction to box breathing. It's called that because as you do it, you can trace a box with your fingers across to the right, down, back to the left and up. This will cause your lungs to slowly expand and your heart to slow down. This will send a feeling of calmness throughout your nervous system, and your vagus nerve will send out the calming chemical acetylcholine. It is called box breath as you can trace a box while doing each step to help you time your breath. You can then use this visualization in the future to help you pace your breath under pressure.

Box breathing in five steps:

1. Inhale for a count of four.

2. Hold for a count of four.

3. Exhale for a count of four.

4. Wait for a count of four.

5. Repeat.[42]

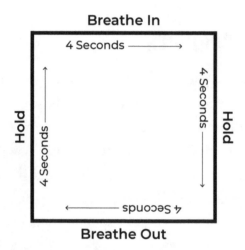

BELLY BREATHING

Breath is your secret weapon, your never-fail remedy.

Dr. Katherine Rosa of the Harvard-affiliated Benson-Henry Institute for Mind Body Medicine says you should breathe like a sleeping child, from the belly and not the chest.

I'll make a guess that you're a chest breather. Many of us in this stressful world are, and we gulp air to escape, not from wild animals any longer, but from real-life threats and stressors.

Like the box breathing exercise above, belly breathing stimulates the vagus nerve and activates your relaxation response. Here's how to experience it:

---

42   Asprey, "How to Strengthen Your Vagus Nerve."

While sitting in a chair, lean forward, place your elbows on your knees, and breathe naturally. You will then know how it feels to breathe from your belly. Another way, what Dr. Rosa calls "the mini," is to take three slow, deep belly breaths. With one hand on your belly and one hand on your chest, breathe, making sure only the hand on your belly is moving in and out.[43]

My clients often find it a challenge to connect mind with body awareness in this exercise; they are unsure whether they are doing it properly. This visual check can be helpful.

- Step 1: You can initially train your body to do this while lying down. Place a stuffed animal or light object on your tummy. Breathe deeply into your belly button, filling your body with air. You will see the object move upward. When releasing your breath, try to have the object go to the lowest possible point (i.e., empty your lungs). Do this a few times with your eyes open to bring awareness to what your abdomen feels like in each position. Watch the object go to the highest and lowest point and connect your mind with how your body feels when it does so. Repeat without the object.
- Step 2: Do this exercise with your eyes closed; try to feel the same expansions and contractions within as you fill and empty your lungs.
- Step 3: Do this exercise sitting.
- Step 4: Do this exercise standing.

When doing this exercise in nonstressful moments, you can train your body to default to this powerful breath in stressful times. My

---

43   Matthew Solan, "Ease Anxiety and Stress: Take a (Belly) Breather,"
      Harvard Health Blog, April 26, 2019, https://www.health.harvard.edu/blog/
      ease-anxiety-and-stress-take-a-belly-breather-2019042616521.

clients find this information empowering, and so do I. Whether giving a speech or presenting an idea to a colleague or family member, you don't have to play Russian roulette with anxiety and cortisol. Instead, you can learn to control both through your breathing. Connect your mind and body and your voice will follow.

4-7-8 HOT CHOCOLATE

This 4-7-8 tool is a powerful one. It reminds you to know what's going on in your body (cortisol, nervousness, anxiety), so you can decrease it with your breath pattern. That's the 4-7-8 part. This mental cue reminds you to breathe in through your nose (enjoying the smell of hot cocoa)—to the count of four—hold your breath to a count of seven, and then, blow it out on an imaginary hot chocolate (as if you are cooling it) to the count of eight. (The order is important as doing it in reverse can make you feel unwell.)

POP!

This is a game to induce cortisol within your system. This is best done with a friend or group. You can use an aid like a "Phlat ball," which you can press together; it will expand and "pop" open causing a startle reflex in whoever catches the ball. (If you are alone, close your eyes and hold the ball until it opens and then proceed.) After you've been startled, use the Hot Chocolate 4-7-8 exercise to calm yourself down as you create a timed speech on a random object in the room. You can increase the speech length from 45 seconds to 1.5 minutes or longer as you become more adept at controlling your breath while producing coherent speeches.

SELF-AWARENESS AND NEUROPLASTICITY

What we're really talking about here is self-regulation. You can't regulate yourself until you have self-awareness, and that is one of my major goals with my clients and with you. As you become more aware of both your emotional and physiological states, you will also become more aware of when and how to use the tools in this book.

Looking forward can only happen if you are willing to look back and to be authentic. Doing so allows you to record where you are in your history, being honest with yourself. You are only accountable to yourself as you develop awareness and self-regulation. You need to see yourself from the inside out.

Start by being more present. This requires emotional intelligence. Don't view your areas of development as weaknesses but as areas you can change for the better. You can do this by looking at it as "We don't know what we don't know." Curiosity brings humility. But how do you develop awareness? I truly believe that skill is a superpower, and many have no idea what an amazing power it is. Self-awareness brings about self-measurement, and from that comes self-regulation.

You can do this for yourself, and the practice will get easier over time. When you're a passenger in a car, you don't pay attention to the directions and the street signs. If you rely on Google Maps and Siri, how long will it be before you lack the ability to sit down and plan a trip without them? I remember when I used to map out a road trip right down to the pit stops for food and gas. As much as I appreciate being able to do all that faster now, faster isn't always better (or even always more accurate), and anything that contributes to the dumbing down of our culture may not be as useful as it appears.

Thus, you need to know how to monitor yourself, just as many of us do when we work out at our gyms without needing to depend on any tech watches. Trust yourself, and when you practice self-monitoring, you'll be able to. You are actually training and retraining your brain.

You can use this Known-Unknown Matrix[44] to track your self-awareness development:

	KNOWNS	UNKNOWNS
KNOWNS	**KNOWN KNOWNS** Things we are aware of and understand	**KNOWN UNKNOWNS** Things we are aware of, but don't understand
UNKNOWNS	**UNKNOWN KNOWNS** Things we understand but are not aware of	**UNKNOWN UNKNOWNS** Things we are neither aware of nor understand

In the journey toward enhanced communication skills, the Known-Unknown Matrix emerges as a powerful tool for cultivating self-awareness. This framework, traditionally employed in knowledge assessment, is ingeniously adaptable for personal development in communication. It categorizes your competencies and awareness into four distinct quadrants:

---

44   Miro, "Constantin Kichinsky's Known-Unknown Matrix Template," Miro, https://miro.com/miroverse/knownunknown-matrix-69w3bdmau9ayprzn/.

1. Known Knowns (Aware Strengths): This quadrant contains the communication skills you consciously recognize as your strengths. Embracing and honing these known strengths enables you to leverage them more effectively in your interactions.

2. Known Unknowns (Acknowledged Weaknesses): Here lie the skills or areas in communication you are aware you lack. This awareness is crucial, as it forms the foundation for targeted improvement through training, mentorship, or self-study.

3. Unknown Knowns (Unrealized Strengths): These are your hidden assets—communication skills you possess but haven't fully recognized. Identifying these requires introspection, feedback from others, and keen attention to your interactions, enabling you to bring these latent strengths to the fore.

4. Unknown Unknowns (Blind Spots): The most elusive quadrant, it represents aspects of your communication style that you are completely unaware of. These blind spots can significantly impact your interactions and are often uncovered through deep self-exploration, guided by feedback from trusted colleagues or through professional assessments.

By employing the Known-Unknown Matrix, you embark on a path of self-discovery and skill enhancement. This journey not only refines your communication abilities but also fosters more effective, empathetic, and meaningful interactions in both your personal and professional life.

In chapter 3, we learned that growth mindset research shows that we are, in fact, capable of "rewiring" our brain and skill sets by virtue of neuroplasticity. This knowledge is crucial to you as a speaker. If you can apply growth mindset language toward your self-awareness, in the context of this matrix, this is a superpower that will push you to greatness. When you are presenting information, you want to retain that information and access impactful vocabulary while being aware, at the same time, of what is happening to you neurologically. That self-awareness will lead you to self-monitoring.

Your goal is to instigate a dopamine response in your audience while monitoring yourself as you speak. In order to balance all the functions that are underway internally, you ultimately need to control your mind through complex territory. And you can.

Remember that stress—and most definitely cortisol—are not logical. Regardless of how real they seem, they are often only primitive, instinctive responses to imaginary dangers.

THE GREAT EQUALIZER: CORTISOL LEVELS RISE, REGARDLESS OF PREPARATION

You've heard the expression "The bigger they are, the harder they fall." This is not the case with cortisol. It is an equal opportunity destroyer—if you're not prepared, that is.

I believe that once you view yourself as being in a "state" rather than "being labeled a certain way" and understand the science behind your inner self, you can then control that self and exude confidence. *If you perceive a situation to be less stress-inducing, you can better control your cortisol response and decrease your physiological reactions in this context.*

So this leads us to question *how* we can change our perception of stressful situations.

As an observer, I have always found myself analyzing people around me to see how they react verbally and nonverbally in stressful situations and wonder to myself what is it that is triggering them or alternately why they appear so calm and collected. I have learned that it often comes down to this key element: *perception of the environment and the ability to control one's mindset in that environment—in an instant.*

As I was writing this book, I was fortunate to have attended four executive education programs at Harvard Business School, where I met a brilliant bunch of professors and fellow students. I was excited to hear what they had to say.

Even more so, I was so intrigued by the method each professor used to engage discussion in our sessions. I was fully aware that that moment of being called upon can be so daunting to those who are not accustomed to such a format. Two professors, Professor Dutch Leonard and Professor and Vice Provost Bharat Anand, particularly stood out in my mind as being able to elicit the best from students and thread together fabulous frameworks that could then be applied in the business contexts. They were masterful in their humility of sharing their knowledge while empowering others to contribute maximally to the class conversation and test their personal understanding of case facts.

Many law and business schools are known for engaging students using the Socratic method. To some, this triggers fear of judgment which may be layered deep within due to some insidious feedback, comments remarked years in the past. It might have been related to observations about one's assertiveness, the way they dress, your apparent demeanor, your cultural background. The effects of these comments covertly remain within us and affect our confidence later in life. Students of such programs comment that they were absolutely petrified about the Socratic method because they were not comfortable with public speaking. What amazes me was that when they offered their ideas, they had the most brilliant critical analyses, yet would not have shared them had they not stepped out of their comfort zone and spoken up in sessions. I empathized with their struggles to express themselves as I flashed back to law school and recalled the early days of how many of us had to become adept at being called on in class—ready to analyze cases from both perspectives, under pressure, at the drop of a hat.

And the experiences of these students weren't unusual. Approximately 85 percent of students experience stress from giving class presentations and most academic pressures. There was an interesting study on this conducted at Molloy College in New York. An experiment was conducted to determine whether there is a correlation between increased preparedness, sleep, level of understanding, perceived anxiety, and physiological stress parameters. Compared to baseline, cortisol levels on the day of the presentation were significantly increased in students who prepared and those who did not. The change in salivary cortisol levels did not correlate with the number of hours spent preparing, the level of understanding, or hours of sleep the night before the presentation. However, students who felt ambiguous toward their level of understanding of their presentation experienced lower changes in cortisol levels. In other words, those who didn't care literally didn't sweat it.

This study suggests that undergraduates' perceived stress in anticipation of public speaking did indeed manifest in significantly elevated cortisol levels. It did not provide a link between increased preparation and reduction of stress parameters.[45]

I could have told you the results of this study because I see it every day in the people I guide, regardless of their academic or professional success. Stress is the great equalizer. I hope you have gathered that stress is highly influenced by mindset. Let us pause and remind ourselves that a regulated and intentioned mindset will shift our perspective and sense of control over any given scenario. Try to remember

---

45   Jodi F. Evans et al., "The Stress of Public Speaking Increases Cortisol Levels in Undergraduates: Is Increased Preparation Really the Best Remedy?," (poster), presented at the 29th Annual Convention of the Association for Psychological Science, Boston, MA, 2017.

that an overwhelming rush of cortisol that feels as if it is going to overcome you with anxiety isn't the end. It's merely a symptom that—by the time you finish the book and begin your journal—you will know how to control.

I refer you back to page 43 for some examples of how to shift from a fixed mindset to a growth mindset when you are feeling stress.

INSTEAD OF SAYING	SAY
My body does all these funny things when I am nervous.	Those funny feelings are merely instinctive responses.
My body fights me when I need to present.	I can retrain my body and brain to change their reaction to stress.
I get this feeling when called on in a meeting.	I am in control of these physiological responses/reactions and will not allow them to hijack my opportunity to shine.
When I get nervous, my fears are all I can think about.	My fears are based on past situations that remind me of this one. I am in a fresh moment.
When I look at the audience, I sweat and forget what to say.	I acknowledge my nerves and breathe deeply, reminding myself that all is well.
I was ridiculed in school when I had to give a speech, and I'm afraid that will happen again.	These feelings are based on what happened in the past. I can feel them but not let them control me.

MINDSET IMPACT ON CORTISOL EXERCISE

Let's try an activity. I am purposely not giving you any context. Grab a pencil and a timer. Use this speech bubble. Set the timer to forty-five seconds. (It is even better if you can ask someone to start the timer for you.) Once the timer starts, write as many words that start with the first letter of your name as you can. If you want to challenge yourself further, choose only adjectives or only nouns.

REFLECTIONS:

Number of words: _____

Physical reactions I felt during this exercise:

_____

_____

_____

_____

My mindset regarding completing this exercise:

_____

_____

_____

_____

What worked and what I could have done better:

_____

_____

_____

_____

This activity is very useful, as it triggers what happens to many in public speaking situations. There is a time limit, you have a message to share, and pressure is added. Despite it being a simple exercise, often clients say their minds go blank. This is because our bodies shut down, and "brain freeze" sets in when cortisol spikes. Mindset and cortisol release are interconnected. Control your mindset, use the exercises to control your cortisol release, and you will be off to a great start.

I did this exact activity at a recent conference that brought together people from all corners of the world. Once the time was up, they had to count how many words they had, and then line their papers up in a row from the least number of words to the greatest number. This was not intended to be a competitive exercise.

I then asked individuals to reflect, in one or two words, how they felt under pressure, and I was fascinated at seeing and then hearing a literal spectrum of responses to the cortisol that had been induced in the seventy attendees. Many said their minds went completely blank, accompanied by a varied rush of physiological sensations. Those who viewed the opportunity as an exciting challenge had been able to write down more words than those who experienced self-doubt or fear in the moment. So what does that mean? Does fear hinder self-expression? Does a positive mindset allow for greater creativity? How did it affect you?

DIFFERENT NEEDS, DIFFERENT RESULTS

Remember, the journey is varied—this development journey is personal to you, your current state, your history. You need to customize this book and the exercises I present here to your very specific needs based on your current psychological state, your personality, your current anxiety level—and your current self-awareness level. Numerous elements come together to create communication intelligence, and you could be anywhere on that spectrum. But the results you will get, regardless of where you are on that spectrum, are assured. All the tools and tracking methods you need are in this book.

In the next chapter, we're going to examine a personality trait that can help you reach your goals.

KEY TAKEAWAYS

1. **Understanding stress response.** The brain responds to perceived threats by triggering an emotional response in the limbic system. The hypothalamus then warns the adrenal glands, which release adrenaline and cortisol, causing physical symptoms of stress.

2. **Controlling stress with mindset and breath.** Understanding and accepting these reactions as automatic can help to control them. Stress can be managed by changing our mindset and controlling our physiological responses, particularly through focused breathing.

3. **The importance of self-awareness and self-regulation.** Self-awareness is the key to managing stress responses and enhancing emotional intelligence. By developing self-awareness and monitoring our own emotional and physiological states we can begin to self-regulate and rewire our brain's responses to stress.

CHAPTER 7

From Grit to Gravitas

It's not that I'm so smart, it's just that I stay with problems longer.

—ALBERT EINSTEIN

I wish I could simply hand you the next three chapters and send you happily into the world of communication. Moreover, I wish possessing the tools in this book was all it would take for you to become a master communicator. Over the years, I have learned that knowledge of what to do is simply not enough.

Picture this scenario: You're an expert in your field. You know that by mastering communication intelligence, you will be able to achieve the state of flow that will allow you to effortlessly deliver your message to any audience, regardless of size, on demand, or at the drop of a hat. In short, communication intelligence (CQ) is a game-changer for you, the ingredient you've been seeking. Then, you have in your hands the very tools you need, along with the journal to record your practicing these tools. In only a few minutes a day, every day, you will be this much closer to mastery. That's all you have to do. Practice.

What happens? You don't show up.

That's right. In my experience, the place where most otherwise disciplined people falter is in the follow-through. They mean to practice the exercises. They intend to practice the exercises. They don't practice the exercises. I'm telling you this not to discourage you, but to help you avoid falling into that trap; the quality of grit can help you do that. It is not enough to simply practice from time to time. Rather, you need to practice with intention and commitment over time. The secret sauce is what I call Communication Grit.

PASSION AND PERSEVERANCE

In *Grit: The Power of Passion and Perseverance*, a book I mentioned earlier, Angela Duckworth says that talent does not guarantee success, and she shares scientific evidence that the personality trait she labels "grit" can grow. In impressive studies with such diverse groups as Green Berets, teachers, sales representatives, and National Spelling Bee contestants, she shows how grit, that combination of passion and perseverance, differs from ability, even outstanding ability.

This is how she explains it: "Talent is how quickly your skills improve when you invest effort. Achievement is what happens when you take your acquired skills and use them. Of course, your opportunities—for example, having a great coach or teacher—matter tremendously, too."[46]

If this sounds like just another pep talk about trying harder, think again. In Duckworth's research, grit comes up again and again as the quality that makes the difference between success and failure, and the good news is that it's not the same as being born with a gift

---

46 Angela Duckworth, *Grit: The Power of Passion and Perseverance* (New York: Simon & Schuster/Paula Wiseman Books, 2016), 42.

for mastering math or writing sonnets. It's something that can be developed.

GRIT AND STOICISM

Grit is what keeps us from giving up. It requires four psychological assets: interest, the capacity to practice, purpose, and hope. You must want the goal you've chosen. You have to be willing to practice to achieve it. You need a good, solid reason for wanting your goal, and you need to have hope that you can get there. Changing the way you communicate will require all of these; it's such a basic aspect of who you are that it will take deep work to manifest abilities that have been forced to go undercover because of what's happened to you.

To those four assets, let's add something we discussed in chapter 3: stoicism, the ability to live happily, striving for rationality and health. When you combine the determination of grit with stoicism, you have a winning combination.

Let's say your goal is to inspire action to better the world through your speaking. Since you were young, you have wanted to have a positive impact on the world, and in your current job, for a company that promotes green technologies, you are about to start speaking to groups about converting to such technologies. You know you need help with the nerves that rise when you even consider becoming the center of attention: You've always thrived working quietly in the background, getting lots of things done but not drawing notice to yourself. This new work scares you, but you know you will grow, and you are determined to commit to the time needed to work through your difficulties. You hope that at long last, you can truly be the person you know you are inside. It looks like you might just have the grit you need to take this on. And in fact, you exhibit signs of stoicism as well;

you are happy and excited to embark on this journey of reclaiming your truest self.

But it's not always that easy, is it? Duckworth asks, "How often do people start down a path and then give up on it entirely? How many treadmills, exercise bikes, and weight sets are at this very moment gathering dust in basements across the country? … How many of us start something new, full of excitement and good intentions, and then give up—permanently—when we encounter the first real obstacle, the first long plateau in progress?"[47]

Duckworth makes a strong point that "skipping around from one kind of pursuit to another—from one skill set to an entirely different one—that's not what gritty people do."[48]

TEN THOUSAND HOURS? START WITH SIX WEEKS

Like Malcolm Gladwell in *Outliers* (in which he examines the conditions of success for the Beatles, Bill Gates, Steve Jobs, and others), Duckworth emphasizes the importance of practice. The optimal is at least twenty hours of practice a week over a ten-year period, for a total of ten thousand hours. This is based on research by K. Anders Ericsson,[49] who found that experts do an intensive kind of practice called deliberate practice.

I'm not going to ask that much of you. If you will give me six weeks of your time, seven days a week—a very small percentage of

47 Duckworth, *Grit*, 50.

48 Duckworth, *Grit*, 54.

49 Samphy, "Deliberate Practice by Anders Ericsson: What It Is And How Can You Deliberately Practice Something," Y Samphy (blog), June 18, 2021, https://www.ysamphy.com/anders-ericsson-deliberate-practice/.

your day, maybe even while you are driving—I can help you master communication intelligence and achieve a state of flow.

If you are questioning yourself, let me share an experience that will hopefully shift your perspective. In my recent visit to Barry's, an iconic fitness studio renowned for its high-intensity workouts, I came across a quote that profoundly resonated with me: "Objects in this mirror are stronger than they may appear." This statement, found in a place celebrated for transforming physical strength and endurance, struck a deep chord within me, particularly in its relevance to the journey of honing communication skills.

Barry's is not just a gym; it's a temple of transformation where individuals push their physical limits under the guidance of expert trainers, amid pulsating music and a motivational ambiance. It's a place where every drop of sweat and every moment of exertion contributes to building not just muscle, but also character and resilience.

This setting, where physical and mental boundaries are continuously challenged and expanded, perfectly encapsulates the essence of developing communication skills. Just as our physical strength often surpasses what we perceive in the mirror, our capacity to communicate effectively often exceeds our own self-assessment.

Our mindset, whether in the adrenaline-fueled environment of Barry's or in the journey of mastering communication, is a vital determinant of our progress. When we question our abilities, whether in executing a challenging workout or articulating complex thoughts, we limit our potential. Yet, if we approach these challenges with the conviction that we are more capable than we initially think, we unlock a level of perseverance and resilience essential for growth.

The analogy of the mirror in Barry's, reflecting back a version of ourselves engaged in physical transformation, parallels our journey in developing communication skills. Just as the mirror might not fully capture the extent of our physical capabilities, our self-view might not accurately reflect our communicative competence. However, with a growth-oriented mindset and a belief in our inherent capabilities, we can transcend these perceived limitations.

In essence, the environment of Barry's, characterized by its dynamic energy and relentless pursuit of improvement, serves as a powerful metaphor for the journey in communication skill development. It reminds us that our perceptions are often just a shadow of our true potential, in fitness, in communication, and in life. Take your first step with me and I promise you will not regret it.

FIVE CORE CHARACTER TRAITS

Which people are grittier? Do you perhaps possess more grit than that smug competitor who's always posting his or her successes, cars, and vacations all over social media? Perhaps. According to Duckworth, "Gritty people aren't monks, nor are they hedonists. In terms of pleasure-seeking, they're just like anyone else; pleasure is moderately important no matter how gritty you are. In sharp contrast, you can see that grittier people are dramatically more motivated than others to seek a meaningful, other-centered life. Higher scores on purpose correlate with higher scores on the Grit Scale."[50]

The big question I'm asked on a daily basis is, "How do I achieve a complete transformation of my communication skills when I've been acting, speaking, and interacting a certain way my entire life? Can you just give me a quick fix to make things change?"

I will share with you what I share with all my clients: It takes hard work and commitment and very simply communication grit. The only

---

50 Angela L. Duckworth et al., "Grit Scale," PsycTESTS Dataset, January 1, 2007, https://doi.org/10.1037/t07051-000.

way to transform your default method of communicating is to spend consistent time periods focused on improving specific elements of your communication message. Many have heard of the "six weeks to habit" approach. In my perspective these six weeks are, in the grand scheme of things, a quick fix.

If you're so inclined, you may want to consider your personality tendencies. In fact, since the days of ancient Greece, people have been trying to figure out the differences in personality. As you will see below, there are five characteristics you can reflect upon. This is a good starting point for your self-awareness journey and goal-setting exercises below.

What is known as the Big Five began when researcher Lewis Goldberg reduced Raymond Cattell's sixteen "fundamental factors" of personality into five primary factors,[51] similar to the five factors found by psychology researchers in the 1960s. They are openness, conscientiousness, extroversion, agreeableness, and neuroticism.

Are some of the Big Five a better grit fit than others? Perhaps when looking at a group of people, but you are an individual, and when you take control of your mindset—and you can—you can take the next step to grit. Specifically linked to communication skills, grit requires a daily inner voice modification where you mindfully reword sentences related to the following:

- Your mindset related to your confidence
- Your mindset related to stressful situations
- The goals you are trying to achieve in a communication context or opportunity
- Kindness toward oneself when one doesn't achieve the goal intended

---

51   "Big 5 Personality Traits," *Psychology Today*, January 17, 2022, https://www.psycholo-gytoday.com/us/basics/big-5-personality-traits.

- A learning goal from each communication scenario that is
  presented and a reflection of what did and/or did not work
  and why

While you can set these goals for yourself as a practical way to
rewire your inner voice for communication grit, the concept comes
to life through your language choice. Certain phrases promote a
fixed communication mindset, whereas language shifts as noted will
empower you to achieve your goals through a communication growth
mindset that is underpinned and fueled by stoicism.

GOAL	FIXED MINDSET PHRASE	COMMUNICATION GROWTH MINDSET PHRASE
Your mindset related to your confidence	I must be the worst speaker on the planet.	I may not be a strong speaker yet; however I'm a strong person for choosing to face this challenge.
Your mindset related to stressful situations	I was so scared I couldn't even think, never mind speak coherently.	I was surely overwhelmed in the moment, but I am so happy I remembered to use the breath techniques I learned! That was better than last time.
The goals that you are trying to achieve in a communication context or opportunity	Everyone in the audience looks so much smarter than I am.	I am so impressed by the credentials of those in the audience, and honor myself for deciding to speak and share what I am passionate about. I deny the power of the voices in my head.
Kindness toward oneself when one doesn't achieve the goal intended	Well, that was a complete disaster.	Well, that was an excellent learning opportunity. While I feel much more confident in how I did X, next time I will ...
A learning goal from each communication scenario that is presented		What did I learn from this presentation? What did not work in this meeting? What reaction did I receive? What needs to be shifted next time?

As you will note, a successful completion of this type of gritty execution to your communication messages requires intention, self-awareness in the moment, and self-kindness. Remember this regardless of whether you are speaking to someone else—or yourself.

IS GRIT ALL YOU NEED?

Of course not. It isn't all you need in real life, and it isn't all you need to achieve communication intelligence.

In addition to serving corporate clients and being the mother of four, I have been blessed to work with thousands of children and shine a light on the importance of integrating communication skills as a core life skill in education. In my work with children, teaching them communication skills, I see the importance of mindset, and as I've mentioned earlier in this book, I've witnessed how easily a parent, teacher, elder, or bully can build or destroy that mindset in a simple sentence or a fleeting moment. I see how these mindsets persist into the personalities of my adult clients, plaguing them with self-doubt. Cultural sensitivities, personality-linked statements, events in the classroom can, in a flash, rob you of your confidence, and slap on a seemingly permanent label. You may be able to identify them later in life and sort through the layers of misconstrued scenarios that unnecessarily held you back from rising to your true potential; you may start your journey to developing your CQ moment by moment, conversation by conversation, meeting by meeting, negotiation by negotiation.

With a stoic mindset, both child and adult will find an easier path to communication grit. With grit, both will be able—and disciplined enough—to practice the tools of communication intelligence. Think of it this way. Your destination is flow. The vehicle to get you there is communication intelligence. The fuel that drives that vehicle is grit.

For speakers, grit helps you become more mindful. It also improves your ability to self-assess; think of it as your true north on your internal compass. In a way, it is what you're relying on when, in the act of speaking, you observe your thoughts and change them despite what you're feeling, physiologically or emotionally, in the moment. If you waver off your goal, feel how the magnetic force "communication grit" pulls you to your true north goal statement. More important though, it's what will keep you practicing those tools in chapters 8, 9, and 10 until they're part of you. I say more important because if you push through and make those tools your own, you will be able to observe your thoughts—and your actions—in real time while you are engaged in communication.

As major as mindfulness and self-assessment are, a key factor to mastery is your absolute refusal to give up. That's because you shift your internal dialogue (I'm sweating, I'm nervous, please, just don't let me pass out) to something like this: Yes I'm going to improve. I have hacked myself. This is an autonomous physiological response. I am in control of my mind, body, and voice. I'm going to have a growth mindset, and I'm going to be very specific in which skills I'm going to improve. I'm going to be mindful on a daily basis, seven days a week—and this is how I'm going to track myself—in this journal.

Grit really comes into play when you continue to fail, which you may at first, and you keep going and are able to maintain that commitment to improving so that you ultimately deliver sustained results. Your purpose is not to just have a successful presentation or an effective conversation or a positive effect on one of your team members. The point is to shift your natural ability and overall communication intelligence quotient so that you are functioning at a higher baseline than you were before you picked up this book.

SUCCESS STORY

You'll remember a client I mentioned earlier. He was tapped to move from the Middle East to lead a team in London.

This executive had an accent that he was self-conscious of and was concerned it may impact his initial transition into a more senior role in London. He was highly self-aware of which syllables he felt he had trouble enunciating and felt he needed to overcome his natural physiology of articulation which arose from his mother tongue. When I first explained the science of communication to him and emphasized how the content of his message compared to the importance of his delivery, he literally put his head in his hands and shook his head, because he understood right away what I was telling him.

"Oh my gosh, are you serious?" he said. "That's my worst part. I know it."

I could feel his self-awareness come into play, and it was one of those moments most of us have had where, all this time, you thought you were great at something, and then you realized how much work you had ahead of you. It was a very poignant, honest experience for him and for me as his guide. By becoming more mindful through discipline, he learned the physiology of articulation and, yes, through grit never missed a night of his tasks that were assigned.

This executive was huge in terms of his commitment—a true superstar. We already knew his articulation was a priority goal, and he followed the exercises on a nightly basis and ended up in an even higher position in the firm's London office. He checked in with me daily asking for strategies on how to refine certain syllables. He was determined, so self-analytical. He went from self-conscious and concerned about the new position in this move to leading this team in a culturally different environment and was completely empowered with his narrative, with his body language, and with his articulation. To see how clients like him supercharge their profession using this method reaffirms my purpose and mission.

FILL UP BEFORE YOU SPEAK UP

I've devoted a chapter to grit for a reason. It's the metaphorical gas in the tank, and as I mentioned earlier, too many people don't take the time to fill up. They're a lot like those drivers who see the needle creeping toward "empty" on the gas gauge but tell themselves and others, "I'm too busy right now. I'll take care of this later." Then, before you know it, "later" arrives, and there they are, unprepared and stranded. I don't want that for you. I wrote this book so that you would not ever again have to be stranded on a stage, in a meeting or a negotiation. I want you to sail through that important presentation as effortlessly as do those with unlimited charisma and years of experience. At least, I want you to appear to.

As I've said, my goal in this book is to help you achieve a state of flow, and that isn't something you're going to magically wake up with in the morning. It's not something you can purchase, and it's not something you can pretend to embody. If you can make time for it, it is in your power to transform authentically and naturally so that when you speak you are in your true essence.

So make the time, all right? I often get told by my clients that they wish I could sit on their shoulder like a little bird and guide them in the moment with all the tools they learn. That will be the effect if you embrace these practical lessons and integrate them into your daily routines.

It's the only way you can be certain you will get where you want to go as a communicator. You can have all the skills in the world, but without that grit and unless you are committed to and have a disciplined approach to it, they're just skills.

You may not yet understand the level of mastery and transformation of which you are capable, but I do. That's my job and my passion, and I can assure you that if you do as I ask in the following chapters, you—like the client I described above—are going to master communication intelligence and achieve flow.

Now that I've shared with you how you need to learn, I'm going to share with you the heart of what you need to learn. Are you ready? More important, are you gritty and ready to be stoic? If so, let's take a look at those tools that can change your communication intelligence and your life.

CHAPTER 8

Your CQ Checklist—Content

No matter what people tell you, words and ideas can change the world.

—ROBIN WILLIAMS

A nine-year-old girl stands before the video camera. She speaks to it, to her audience, not to the charts and graphs beside her. Effortlessly, she gives her presentation on—what else?—giving a successful speech. She doesn't stutter, doesn't fill her talk with filler words. She just presents her information in a clear, calm, resonant voice.

If a nine-year-old can do it, so can you.

Recently, one of my clients proudly told me that she had memorized all of my presentation tools and went over them one by one when giving an important speech. Although learning all the tools is part of the process, it's not the goal. Mastery is. That's what you'll learn in this chapter—the individual tools that will become so natural you won't have to think about them.

Let's get real. It's great to read about all of these theories and understand the science, but it's time to put theories into action—and give you a path to success. If you will invest six weeks, I can help you do that. Although you will not master all the tools you will learn in this chapter overnight, you will definitely see improvement. Once you spend those six weeks practicing, you will begin to achieve flow, which is a very different level of mastery than skills development alone. Six weeks. That's not even a semester! Are you willing to commit that time to achieving your goal?

These practices are based on heavily researched data, and I'm presenting them to you in the form of a pre-presentation checklist that includes a series of exercises. In the back of this book, you will find your own journal, where you can plan—and track—a week at a time. And you will need to do both! Different speaking opportunities will require you to develop and depend on different tools.

Suppose you have an important meeting scheduled. Or perhaps you need to make a presentation, proposal, pitch, or speech. You know that you want to improve your vocal image, specifically with respect to speaking with authority. That is when you reach for your communication journal. You can't follow a workout plan until you learn how to plan how many leg extensions you need or how many calf raises or squats. To my mind, how you present yourself as a communicator is just as crucial, and it's a skill that won't just take care of itself.

Some of you, of course, will not have a specific presentation or speaking event that you are currently working toward. I invite you to intentionally create moments to practice the skills learned below and test yourself in the moment. I will nudge you along the way.

COLUMN ONE: 7 PERCENT—CONTENT

7% CONTENT, STRUCTURE, VOCABU-LARY, PERSUASION ("WHAT YOU SAY")	38% INTONATION, ARTICULATION ("HOW YOU SAY IT")	55% NONVERBAL COMMUNICATION ("HOW YOU SAY IT")

When we are considering column 1 of our CQ pre-presentation checklist (CQPPC), we should bear in mind that content has different elements, including the following:

1. Structure of your speech
2. Literary devices that impact
3. Persuasive modes and strategies
4. Vocabulary choice
5. Transitional and impactful phrases

We will look at each of these in turn below.

STRUCTURE OF YOUR SPEECH: MAXIMIZE THIS USING THE SPEECH BURGER

Mental visuals make for powerful reminders when you're in the moment. The image of the speech burger can help you maintain a clear, helpful structure. Use the graphic organizer below as you prepare your speeches or narratives.

In a speech burger, you have four main parts which can be remembered by the acronym ITBC:

I: INTRODUCTION IS THE TOP BUN.

T: TOPPINGS.

B: BURGER.

C: CONCLUSION IS THE BOTTOM BUN.

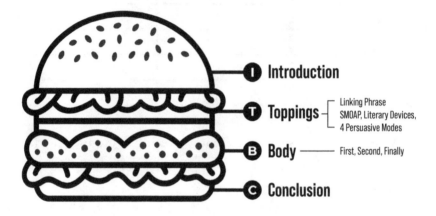

① Introduction

① Toppings ⎡ Linking Phrase
⎢ SMOAP, Literary Devices,
⎣ 4 Persuasive Modes

⑧ Body —— First, Second, Finally

⑥ Conclusion

FISHING FOR AUDIENCE ATTENTION USING FOUR TYPES OF "VERBAL BAIT"

Q: QUESTION HOOK

- Do you want to be...?
- Would you like to...?
- Have you ever <adjective: envisioned, imagined, seen, experienced, believed, felt...> link to an emotion or an experience?

V: VISUAL HOOK

- Connect brain of audience with your words
- Imagine a <noun> that <adjective>

F: FACTOID HOOK

- Hyperbole

M: MATH HOOK

- Apply to your scenario and use relevant data adapted to your argument

S: FIVE SENSES HOOK

- Touch, smell, see, taste, hear
- "Close your eyes" (Link vision)

The top bun is your introduction, including your hook and any introductory marks that build from that hook.

The toppings are factors of speech such as similes, metaphors, onomatopoeia, alliteration, and personification.

The burger is the bulk of the message—what the speaker is knowledgeable about. This is where you let your knowledge shine. When you begin, start with three main points while integrating signposting knowledge to create structure to the flow of your points.

The bottom bun is your conclusion, which is your opportunity to make your final impact and leave the audience wanting more.

THE FOUR COMPONENTS OF
THE SPEECH BURGER

Choose phrases from this chart to start building your speech.

<table>
<tr>
<td rowspan="1">TOP BUN: INTRODUCTION</td>
<td>
Step 1: HOOK—Use any of the QVFMS Hooks
Step 2: What problem will be addressed, and what are you offering as a solution? If an informative speech, what will be covered? Briefly—vision of the road map of your speech. Explain the salient idea (e.g., If you have ever wondered x, I invite you to learn with me today as I show you a new perspective of xyz).
Need to include some language examples where audience is convinced to give their attention for a certain amount of time.
<ul>
<li>My aim is that in the next twenty-five minutes you will transform your perspective on ...</li>
<li>I will demonstrate to you today.</li>
<li>If x is what you are interested in, I invite you to sit, back, relax and enjoy the futuristic revelations I have to share with you today.</li>
</ul>
</td>
</tr>
<tr>
<td>TOPPINGS: DETAILS</td>
<td>
<ul>
<li>For example ...</li>
<li>In fact ...</li>
<li>For instance ...</li>
<li>As evidence ...</li>
<li>In support of this ...</li>
</ul>
· This should include examples of similes, metaphors, onomatopoeia, alliteration, pathos, logos, ethos, and Kairos.
Other toppings of speech
<ul>
<li>Simile: My love is like a red, red rose.</li>
<li>Metaphor: My love is a red, red rose.</li>
<li>Onomatopoeia: Over the rosebush, lightning flashed, and thunder roared.</li>
<li>Alliteration: Red roses remind Riley to remember and reflect.</li>
<li>Personification: The rose unfurled her petals and spoke words of love.</li>
</ul>
</td>
</tr>
<tr>
<td>BURGER: MAKING YOUR POINT</td>
<td>
<table>
<tr><td>· Signposting language</td><td>· Finally ...</td><td>· Surely ...</td></tr>
<tr><td>· Verbal punctuation</td><td>· Likewise ...</td><td>· Certainly ...</td></tr>
<tr><td>· First, second, third ...</td><td>· Besides ...</td><td>· Specifically ...</td></tr>
<tr><td>· Furthermore ...</td><td>· Again ...</td><td>· If ...</td></tr>
<tr><td>· In addition ...</td><td>· Moreover ...</td><td>· then ...</td></tr>
<tr><td>· Also ...</td><td>· Similarly ...</td><td>· because ...</td></tr>
</table>
</td>
</tr>
<tr>
<td>BOTTOM BUN: CONCLUSION</td>
<td>
End Hook: Can be any of the QVFMS Hooks
<table>
<tr><td>· For the reasons stated</td><td>· In short</td><td>· In brief</td></tr>
<tr><td>· As you can see</td><td>· To be sure</td><td>· Undoubtedly</td></tr>
<tr><td>· As I have noted</td><td>· Without a doubt</td><td>· In any case</td></tr>
<tr><td>· In other words</td><td>· Obviously</td><td>· To summarize</td></tr>
<tr><td>· On the whole</td><td>· Unquestionably</td><td>· In any event</td></tr>
</table>
</td>
</tr>
</table>

These elements, while not essential to the audience grasping the meaning of your message, can affect its impact. Think of Dr. Martin Luther King Jr.'s "I Have a Dream" speech, which includes many examples of alliteration, such as "Five score years ago, a great American, in whose symbolic shadow we stand today, signed the Emancipation Proclamation." Take note of those *s* words: score, symbolic, stand, signed, and emancipation (the *s* sound comes in the middle, from the *c*).

Now, read King's statement again, preferably aloud, and pay attention to the sound of the words.

These speech factors are your burger's secret sauce, coloring your wording in a way that makes audiences more excited to hear it. In *The Art of Fiction*,[52] author John Gardner talks about what he calls "psychic distance"—the distance between the reader and the words on the page. The closer the reader feels to the story, the closer the psychic distance. The same is true in communication. The closer each person in the audience feels to you, the more connected they will be.

Besides dressing up the phraseology of a speech, many of these factors have concrete, tested benefits in light of communication. Metaphors, by tapping into audience's familiar experiences, are excellent for shedding light on a topic perceived as cryptic. Alliteration can be a powerful way to help people remember key sayings. Few people, after all, can forget that Sally sells seashells by the seashore—or the lines from King's famous speech above.

Finally, the bottom bun represents the conclusion of the speech, where you try to end on a note as resonant as the one on which you began, preferably tying back to your opening point to make your presentation feel integrated and complete. The way you end a speech depends on the type. A prescriptive (how-to) speech can end by emphasizing how your "prescription" will change the audience

---

52   John Gardner, *The Art of Fiction: Notes on Craft for Young Writers* (Vintage, 1991).

members' lives. An inspirational speech that starts with an "imagine" hook can end by revisiting that hook. If you begin with an anecdote, case history, or even a personal experience—revisit that. You might end with a call to action. "You, I, we need to start … right now." You might end with a look forward: "Start today, and six weeks from now, you will be up here, speaking without fear."

Later, we will look at timing. For now, think of it as if your speech is a real burger. Most of your time will be spent on that meat and making sure that meat is properly spiced and enhanced.

Have you ever started to speak, felt time slow down, wishing you could pull back the words as you were speaking them? Or, alternately, relayed your message perfectly, followed with a feeling of floating on a cloud? Authenticity in language can help strengthen connections and mutual respect. Misplaced words have the effect of being insincere, despite your intentions, and can be a lost opportunity to build a positive relationship. Words have a power frequency; I ask that you remind yourself of this as you construct the content of your message.

GETTING STRATEGIC

Now that you've roughed out your speech, let's look at ways to make it more persuasive.

We'll begin with the acronym PLEK—go ahead, add it to your toolkit. Now, let's learn what Aristotle introduced in his book *Rhetoric*. Having a strong awareness of how to be most convincing to your audience will help you as you speak, as it helps you choose what language to use.

FOUR PERSUASIVE STRATEGIES

1. Pathos

Pathos involves using emotional language that is designed to draw the reader in and make him or her feel for you. It's important to use emotional language authentically and with consideration for the audience. Appealing to pathos can be a powerful way to engage an audience and motivate them to take action. When using emotional language, it's important to be authentic and sincere, and to understand the values and priorities of the target audience. By connecting with an audience on an emotional level, a message can be more memorable and impactful. Appealing to pathos can be effective in certain contexts, but it should be balanced with logical appeals and factual information to create a persuasive message.

- "No price can be placed on peace of mind. Our advanced security systems will protect the well-being of your family so that you can sleep soundly at night."
- "You'll make the right decision because you have something that not many people possess: you have heart."
- "Imagine a world where ..."
- "Think about how you would feel if ..."
- "Don't let this opportunity slip away."
- "You deserve to feel [positive emotion]."
- "Think about the impact you could make."
- "Our product/service can help you achieve your dreams."
- "Join us in making a difference."
- "Together, we can change the world."
- "This is your chance to [desirable outcome]."
- "Let us help you [solve a problem or fulfill a desire]."
- "We believe in making a difference."
- "You can be part of something bigger."
- "Join us in changing the world for the better."
- "Don't miss out on this life-changing opportunity."

- "Let us help you create the life you want."
- "Imagine a world where everyone has access to [insert benefit]."
- "Together, we can create a brighter future."
- "This is more than just a [product/service], it's a way to [insert benefit]."
- "We're passionate about making a positive impact."
- "You're not just investing in [product/service], you're investing in yourself and your future."

2. Logos

Use data, charts, illustrations, and logic to back up your position and points. When using logos appeals, it's important to provide evidence and logical reasoning to back up any claims. This can include statistics, case studies, testimonials, and other forms of proof. The goal is to demonstrate to the audience that your argument or proposal is sound and logical, and that it will deliver the desired results.

- "The data is perfectly clear: this investment has consistently turned a profit year-over-year, even in spite of market declines in other areas."
- "Research compiled by analysts from NASA, as well as organizations from five other nations with space programs, suggests that a moon colony is viable with international support."
- "Based on data and research …"
- "Studies show that …"
- "This is a proven method for achieving [insert benefit]."
- "The numbers speak for themselves."
- "Our approach is based on sound principles of [insert theory]."
- "Our track record speaks for itself."
- "Our solution is the most effective because …"

- "We have a logical and systematic approach to [insert problem]."
- "Our product/service is backed by years of experience."
- "We offer a results-driven solution that [insert benefit]."

3. Ethos

Use language that shows that you as a presenter are trustworthy and believable. These types of words and phrases can help to establish credibility and demonstrate expertise. By appealing to the audience's logical and rational side, you can make a more compelling case for your argument or proposal. Ethos refers to the appeal to ethics or credibility in communication. By appealing to the audience's sense of trust and credibility, these types of words and phrases can help to establish a sense of authority and reliability. This, in turn, can help to persuade the audience to trust and believe in what you are saying. Here are some examples of words and phrases that can appeal to ethos:

- "As a doctor, I am qualified to tell you that this course of treatment will likely generate the best results."
- "My three decades of experience in public service, my tireless commitment to the people of this community, and my willingness to reach across the aisle and cooperate with the opposition make me the ideal candidate for your mayor."
- "As an expert in the field, I can say with confidence that ..."
- "I have [number] years of experience in this industry and have worked on similar projects in the past."
- "Our team includes some of the most respected and knowledgeable professionals in the field."
- "We are committed to ethical and responsible business practices."

- "Our product/service is backed by a guarantee of quality and satisfaction."
- "We have a reputation for excellence and integrity."
- "We take our responsibility to our customers/clients very seriously."
- "We are a trusted and respected leader in the industry."
- "Our company is dedicated to making a positive impact in the world."
- "I have devoted my career to this cause and have seen firsthand the impact it can make."
- "Our organization is dedicated to making a difference in the world, and we have received recognition for our efforts."
- "As a respected leader in the industry, I can tell you that …"
- "Our company has won numerous awards for our innovative and effective solutions."
- "We have a team of experienced professionals who are passionate about what we do and are committed to delivering results."
- "Our product/service has been endorsed by top industry experts."
- "We have a history of delivering on our promises and exceeding our customers/clients' expectations."
- "Our organization is built on a foundation of values such as honesty, integrity, and transparency."
- "We have received positive feedback and testimonials from satisfied customers/clients."
- "Our approach is based on the latest research and best practices in the industry, and we have a track record of success."

4. Kairos

Kairos is a Greek term that refers to the opportune moment or the right time for something. In rhetoric, it is often used to refer to the timing and context of a message. These examples use to emphasize the urgency, importance, and relevance of the message in the current context. By doing so, they create a sense of immediacy and importance that can make the audience more receptive to the message.

SPEECH BURGER

Choose phrases from this chart to start building your speech.

Here are some examples of how Kairos can be used in persuasive communication where the goal is to create a sense of urgency about how this is the right moment to act—a call to action.

- "This is the moment to seize this opportunity. Do you want to live the rest of your years yearning to know what would have happened if you had jumped when you had the chance?"
- "Given the current situation, it's more important than ever that we take action."
- "With this new opportunity, we have the chance to make a real difference."
- "We can't afford to wait any longer to address this issue."
- "This is the moment we've been waiting for to create a better future."
- "In this critical moment, we need to act with urgency and purpose."
- "The timing of our action is crucial to achieving our goals."
- "We have a unique opportunity to make history and be remembered for our impact."
- "The context of this situation demands immediate and decisive action."
- "The stars have aligned for us to make a lasting impact and create meaningful change."

- "Now is the time for us to come together and make a change in our community. With recent events, we have a unique opportunity to address systemic issues and create a better future."
- "As we prepare for the upcoming election, it's more important than ever that we educate ourselves on the issues and make our voices heard. The future of our country depends on it."
- "With the current state of the economy, we have the chance to invest in new industries and create jobs that will benefit our society for years to come. Let's not miss this opportunity."
- "The recent natural disasters have highlighted the need for us to take action on climate change. We can't afford to wait any longer to make the necessary changes."
- "As we enter a new decade, it's time for us to reflect on our past and create a more equitable and just society. The future is in our hands."
- "In the wake of the pandemic, we have a unique opportunity to rebuild our healthcare system and ensure that everyone has access to quality care. Let's seize this moment."
- "The global movement for racial justice has brought attention to the longstanding issues of inequality and discrimination. We must act now to create a more just and equitable society."
- "As we face unprecedented challenges in our world, we have the chance to come together and support each other. This is a time to show compassion and kindness."
- "The advancements in technology have created new opportunities for us to innovate and create a better future. Let's embrace this moment and push the boundaries of what's possible."
- "The world is changing rapidly, and we must adapt to stay relevant. Let's use this moment to learn new skills and explore new possibilities."

TOP BUN: INTRODUCTION	· **Step 1: Hook** · **Step 2: What problem will be addressed, and what are you offering as a solution?** If an informative speech, what will be covered. Briefly—vision of the road map of your speech. Explain the salient idea (e.g., If you have ever wondered *x*, I invite you to learn with me today as I show you a new perspective of *xyz*). Need to include some language examples where audience is convinced to give their attention for a certain amount of time (My aim is that in the next twenty-five minutes, you will transform your perspective on ...] · **Step 3: Get audience to commit their attention to you by using connective phrase language such as:**

TOP BUN: INTRODUCTION	· For this reason ... · I am sure that ... · It is certain ... · Of course ... · In the same way ... · In this situation ... · In my opinion · I believe · It is my belief that · There is no doubt that	· From my point of view · I question whether · I (dis)agree with · I maintain that · I ask you to ... · Think about ... · It has come to my attention that ... · What needs to be done ... · What we need to do

BURGER: MAKING YOUR POINT	· Signposting language · Verbal punctuation · First, second, third ... · Furthermore ... · In addition ... · Also ...	· Finally ... · Likewise ... · Besides ... · Again ... · Moreover ... · Similarly ...	· Surely ... · Certainly ... · Specifically ... · If ... · then ... · because ...
TOPPINGS: DETAILS	· In fact ... · For instance ... · As evidence ... · In support of this ...	· This should include examples of similes, metaphors, onomatopoeia, alliteration, pathos, logos, ethos, Kairos	
BOTTOM BUN: CONCLUSION	· For the reasons stated · As you can see · As I have noted · In other words · On the whole	· In short · To be sure · Without a doubt · Obviously · Unquestionably	· In brief · Undoubtedly · In any case · To summarize · In any event

Now that you've got the basics for crafting your speech, here is the rest of your persuasive phrase toolkit—akin to a language cheat sheet, which will get your creative juices flowing when you face a mental block. You can take any noun and plot it by adding any of these phrases and watch that sentence transform. It is what I call the perfect recipe for persuasion.

PERFECT RECIPE FOR PERSUASION

Practice exercise:

- Level 1: Put on a timer for thirty seconds. Find a random object in the room. Convince a friend why that object is fabulous.
- Level 2: Put on a timer for thirty seconds. This time, choose words from the different column below. Market the same object to your friend using a selection of these ingredients— you now have a perfectly persuasive statement.

TRANSITIONAL PHRASES

SUPPORTING OPINIONS		
· First Furthermore	· Equally important	· Further
· Second Ino addition	· In the first place	· Next Again
· Third Also	· Likewise	· Moreover
· Finally Last	· Besides	· Similarly
CAUSE AND EFFECT		
· Since	· Caused by	· In effect
· Because of	· This results in	· Brought about
· Due to	· Consequently	· Made possible
· For this reason	· Accordingly	· As might be expected
· Therefore	· As a result of	· Give rise to
· If ... then	· Leads to	· Was responsible for

COMPARE AND CONTRAST

· Similarly	· In the same way	· Have in common
· Compared to	· Contrasting	· All are
· In like manner	· On the contrary	· The same as
· On the other hand	· As opposed to	· Conversely
· Although	· Rather than	· Whether or not
· Even though	· Nevertheless	· In spite of
· Likewise	· As well as	

COUNTERING

· I realize you	· Your idea to ___ has merit	· Maintain
· I understand you	· If you move forward	· Want
· Even though you	with ...	· Favor
· Although you	· Regardless ...	· Support
· Some people	· This can be fixed by ...	· Argue
· It may be that you	· Believe	· State
	· Feel	

FOR / AGAINST / PERSUASIVE CALLS TO ACTION

FOR	AGAINST	PERSUASIVE CALLS TO ACTION
· Accurate	· Aggravate	· Because
· Advantage	· Atrocious	· Create
· Always	· Confusing	· Discover
· Beneficial	· Contradictory	· Easy
· Confident	· Costly	· Free
· Definitely	· Damaging	· Guarantee
· Effective	· Disadvantages	· Health
· Emphasize	· Displeased	· Instantly
· Expect	· Dreadful	· Join
· Favorable	· Harmful	· Love
· Greatness	· Harsh	· Must
· Impactful	· Inferior	· Need
· Informative	· Offend	· New
· Magnificent	· Ordeal	· Now
· Most important	· Outrageous	· Only
· Strongly recommend	· Regrettable	· Proven
· Support	· Severe	· Quick
· Strengthen	· Shameful	· Results
· Superior	· Shocking	· Safety
· Workable	· Unreliable	· Save
· Worthwhile	· Unstable	· You

Remember that the subconscious mind does not recognize negatives. Instead of "Don't miss out," pick a positive word from the list, such as *join*, as in "Join now."

Bear in mind the power of three—triples: three words, or even one word repeated three times. "Change we need." "Yes, we can." "Location, location, location."

Once you have mastered the above, you need to decide which persuasive sentence structure applies to your communication context and integrate the vocabulary into one of these structures.

PERSUASIVE SPEECH SENTENCE STRUCTURE	STEPS TO FOLLOW
1. Problem-Solution/ Opportunity	This structure involves identifying a problem and then offering a solution/opportunity. The goal is to convince the audience that your solution is the best one. The structure typically includes: · An introduction that establishes the problem and its significance. · A description of the problem, including evidence to support the claim. · An explanation of the proposed solution or opportunity. · Evidence to support the effectiveness of the solution. · A call to action, urging the audience to support the proposed solution. · Identify an opportunity for growth or progress in solving.
2. Monroe's Motivated Sequence	This structure is a five-step process that aims to motivate the audience to take action. The steps are: · Attention: Capture the audience's attention with a powerful statement or question. · Need: Present the problem and explain why it is important to address it. · Satisfaction: Offer a solution to the problem and explain how it will solve the issue. · Visualization: Use vivid imagery and examples to help the audience imagine the benefits of the proposed solution. · Action: Call to action, urging the audience to take steps to support the solution.

PERSUASIVE SPEECH SENTENCE STRUCTURE	STEPS TO FOLLOW
3. Comparative Advantage	This structure compares two or more options to demonstrate why one is better than the others. The structure typically includes: · An introduction that explains the context and importance of the comparison. · A description of the options being compared. · Evidence and arguments in favor of the preferred option. · Evidence and arguments against the other options. · A conclusion that summarizes the advantages of the preferred option.
4. Refutation	This structure involves anticipating and addressing counterarguments to your position and addressing them before presenting your main points. The structure typically includes: · An introduction that establishes the topic and its significance. · A description of the counterarguments and evidence against your position. · A rebuttal of the counterarguments with evidence and persuasive arguments. · A conclusion that summarizes the strengths of your position and weak points of the counterarguments.
5. Problem-Cause-Solution	This structure identifies the cause of the problem and then presents a solution. The structure typically includes: · An introduction that establishes the problem and its significance. · A description of the problem and its causes. · An explanation of the proposed solution. · Evidence to support the effectiveness of the solution. · A call to action, urging the audience to support the proposed solution.
6. Maslow's Hierarchy of Needs	Structure your argument around Maslow's hierarchy of needs, starting with the most basic needs (e.g., physiological needs) and building up to the highest needs (e.g., self-actualization).
7. Motivation-Action	Begin by motivating your audience to take action on an issue by highlighting the consequences of not acting.
8. Chronological	Present your argument in chronological order to show the evolution of an issue and the importance of your proposed solution.

THE PAINTBRUSH

Whether you are giving a speech or the simplest of presentations, you need to paint a picture for your audience. When you think of this brush, remember the tools at your disposal to paint that picture. Clarity—or clear language—is one of the most important. It's fine to use words in new and vivid ways, but don't use large words or convoluted language in an attempt to impress your audience.

Incorporate the five senses (sight, smell, taste, touch, hearing) in your specificity of language choice. How did the candle smell when you blew it out? How did the door sound when it creaked open in the deserted house? How did the salted caramel ice cream look when the server handed you the cone? How did it taste? These types of word choices have a miraculous impact of connecting with the audience's brain which is tuned to storytelling; this strategy is sure to make you a more memorable speaker.

You aren't just speaking words. You are creating pictures that help your reader experience your message.

Again, I will ask you to pause and bring awareness to the neurochemical impact words can have to affect our emotions and moods based on the sentence structure or syntax you use. For your quick reference, consider the following:

SENTENCE STRUCTURE OR SYNTAX	EXAMPLE	NEUROCHEMICAL IMPACT
Questions	"Have you ever wondered ..." or "How can we improve ..." "Have you considered ..."	Asking questions can create a sense of curiosity and engagement, which can trigger the release of dopamine and norepinephrine in the brain.

SENTENCE STRUCTURE OR SYNTAX	EXAMPLE	NEUROCHEMICAL IMPACT
Repetition of words	"Yes, we can": Barack Obama's campaign slogan in 2008. "I have a dream": repeated by Martin Luther King Jr. during his famous speech. "We shall fight on the beaches, we shall fight on the landing grounds, we shall fight in the fields and in the streets, we shall fight in the hills; we shall never surrender": Winston Churchill's famous speech during World War II.	Repetition of words or phrases can create a sense of rhythm and familiarity, which can trigger the release of dopamine in the brain.
Contrast	"Ask not what your country can do for you, ask what you can do for your country ..." "Sometimes the greatest obstacles can lead to the greatest opportunities." "You can't appreciate the light without experiencing the darkness."	Contrasting ideas or phrases can create a sense of tension and resolution, which can trigger the release of dopamine and norepinephrine in the brain.
Metaphors and analogies	"Life is a journey, not a destination ..." or "She was a ray of sunshine." "She's a firecracker." "The world is your oyster." "Success is like a marathon, requiring endurance and persistence."	Using metaphors or analogies can create a sense of imagery and visualization, which can trigger the release of dopamine in the brain.
Positive affirmations	"I am capable of achieving my goals." "I am worthy of love and respect." "I am strong and resilient." "My voice matters."	Using positive affirmations can create a sense of self-confidence and motivation, which can trigger the release of dopamine and serotonin in the brain.
Negatives	"I'm not saying it's going to be easy, but it will be worth it." "Not only did she overcome adversity, but she also thrived." "We didn't give up, and we succeeded."	Negative sentences can trigger the release of cortisol and create feelings of stress and tension in the brain. However, they can also be used to create a sense of contrast or to emphasize a positive outcome.

SENTENCE STRUCTURE OR SYNTAX	EXAMPLE	NEUROCHEMICAL IMPACT
Inclusive language	"We can do this together." "Let's work together to achieve our goals." "Our team is strong and diverse."	Using inclusive language can create a sense of belonging and community, triggering the release of oxytocin in the brain.
Power words	"Revolutionary" "Inspiring" "Transform" "Conquer" "Empower" "Guaranteed" "Proven" "Exclusive" "Instant" "Sensational" "Incredible" "Phenomenal" "Unsurpassed" "Breakthrough" "Extraordinary" "Remarkable" "Authentic" "Powerful" "Elite" "Epic"	Power words can create a sense of impact and importance, triggering the release of dopamine and norepinephrine in the brain. Keep in mind that power words can be effective when used sparingly and strategically. Using too many of them can make the message come across as exaggerated or insincere. It's important to consider the context and the audience when using power words to create a persuasive message.
Direct questions	"What is your main goal right now?" "How can we work together to achieve our objectives?" "What is the most important thing you need to do today?"	Asking direct questions can create a sense of engagement and focus, triggering the release of dopamine and norepinephrine in the brain.
Juxtaposition	"We have two choices: we can sit back and watch the world go by, or we can take action and make a difference." "The darkness of the night sky was in stark contrast to the bright lights of the city below." "The peacefulness of the countryside was a world away from the chaos of the city."	Juxtaposition: Contrasting and juxtaposing ideas can create a sense of surprise and novelty, triggering the release of dopamine in the brain.

SENTENCE STRUCTURE OR SYNTAX	EXAMPLE	NEUROCHEMICAL IMPACT
Repetition of phrases	"Never give up, never give in, never surrender." "I can do this, I will do this, I am doing this." "It's not how many times you fall down, it's how many times you get back up." "Because you're worth it": L'Oreal's slogan. "Think different": Apple's campaign slogan in the late '90s. "I'm lovin' it": McDonald's slogan. "A diamond is forever": De Beers's slogan. "I want my MTV": A campaign to promote the launch of MTV in the early '80s. "Eat fresh": Subway. "The happiest place on earth": Disneyland's slogan.	Repeating key phrases or ideas can create a sense of emphasis and motivation, triggering the release of dopamine and norepinephrine in the brain.
Hypothetical questions	"What if we could create a world where everyone had access to education and healthcare?" "How would you design a product that solves this problem?" "If you had unlimited resources, what kind of impact could you make?"	Asking hypothetical questions can create a sense of curiosity and creativity, triggering the release of dopamine in the brain.
Imperatives (Kairos)	"Take action now to achieve your goals." "Make a difference in the world today." "Never stop learning and growing."	Using imperatives can create a sense of urgency and motivation, triggering the release of dopamine and norepinephrine in the brain.
Personal anecdotes	"When I faced a similar challenge, here's what worked for me." "I once struggled with this issue myself, and I know how difficult it can be." "Let me tell you a story about how I overcame a major obstacle in my life."	Sharing personal anecdotes can create a sense of empathy and connection, triggering the release of oxytocin in the brain. Using a story to illustrate the benefits of taking a certain action or following a certain path can be very persuasive.

SENTENCE STRUCTURE OR SYNTAX	EXAMPLE	NEUROCHEMICAL IMPACT
Descriptive language	"The sky was ablaze with a stunning array of colors as the sun set in the distance." "The aroma of freshly baked bread filled the air, enticing us with its warm and inviting scent."	Using descriptive language can create a sense of vividness and imagination, triggering the release of dopamine in the brain.
Rhetorical questions	"Who doesn't want to live a fulfilling life?" "Why settle for mediocrity when you can achieve greatness?" "Isn't it time we took action to create a better future?"	Asking rhetorical questions can create a sense of engagement and introspection, triggering the release of dopamine in the brain.
Alliteration	"Galloping gazelles graze on grass." "Wild winds whipped and whirled." "Ripe red raspberries roll around in a basket." "Purring Persian cats play with pink pillows." "A happy hummingbird hovers in the air."	Alliteration is a literary technique that involves the repetition of the initial sounds of words in a sentence or phrase. It is primarily used for stylistic purposes and can create a sense of rhythm, musicality, and emphasis in language. It can have an emotional and aesthetic impact on the audience when the brain processes language and appreciates the beauty of alliteration through the activation of various neural networks, such as the language centers in the left hemisphere and the reward centers in the limbic system.

CREATING TRUST THROUGH LANGUAGE CHOICE

If we think back to the ten-second window and how important it is to grab the audience's attention and trust, this reminds us of the importance of language choice.

NEUROCHEMICAL IMPACT OF WORDS

I want to ask you to pause for a moment and put aside the percentage impact the content can have to rather focus on the neurochemical impact words have on the audience. Recall as noted above that words can impact the neurochemistry of language by triggering the release of neurotransmitters in the brain.

Here are a few examples:

POSITIVE WORDS	Words with positive connotations, such as "love," "happy," "peaceful," and "exciting," can trigger the release of dopamine and serotonin in the brain, which can create feelings of pleasure and happiness.
NEGATIVE WORDS	Words with negative connotations, such as "fear," "anger," "stress," and "hate," can trigger the release of cortisol, which is a stress hormone that can create feelings of anxiety and tension.
EMOTIONAL WORDS	Words that evoke strong emotions, such as "heartbreaking," "exhilarating," "terrifying," and "hilarious," can trigger the release of neurotransmitters such as dopamine and norepinephrine, which can create intense emotional responses.
ACTION WORDS	Words that describe action or movement, such as "run," "jump," "swim," and "dance," can trigger the release of norepinephrine and adrenaline, which can create feelings of excitement and arousal.
SENSORY WORDS	Words that describe sensory experiences, such as "sweet," "salty," "spicy," "fragrant," and "colorful," can activate the brain's sensory cortex and trigger the release of dopamine, which can create feelings of pleasure and satisfaction.

These are just a few examples of how certain words can impact the neurochemistry of language and affect our emotions and moods.

There are different contexts in which you will need to adapt your speech, vocabulary, or language choice. Just as positive and trustworthy language can have a positive impact on the release of oxytocin, the hormone associated with social bonding, trust, and relaxation, I invite you to remember that using language that is clear, personal, active, empathetic, and honest can help create trust in communication. By focusing on these types of language, you can build rapport and understanding with your audience, which can increase their trust in you. By using language that is specific, personal, active, empathetic, and honest, you can build trust and credibility with your communication partners and establish yourself as a trustworthy and reliable person. Here are some examples of types of language that can help create trust in communication:

TRUST-INDUCING LANGUAGE TYPE	IMPACT	EXAMPLE
Concrete language	Use specific and concrete language to convey your message clearly and avoid ambiguity. This helps to build trust by ensuring that the listener understands what you are saying.	"Let's meet at the coffee shop on Main Street at 3:00 p.m.," instead of "We'll get together later."
Personal pronouns	Use personal pronouns, such as "I" and "we," to show accountability and establish a personal connection with the listener. This can increase trust by demonstrating your commitment to the conversation or relationship.	"I appreciate your input on this project," instead of "Your input is appreciated." "We need to work together to solve this problem," instead of "This problem needs to be solved." "We have a shared goal of completing this project on time," instead of "The project needs to be finished by the deadline." "Let's work together to come up with a plan," instead of "You need to figure it out."
Active voice	Use the active voice to show agency and responsibility, and avoid passive or vague language that can be interpreted in different ways. This helps to build trust by demonstrating your confidence and clarity in your communication.	"I will take care of this issue," instead of "This issue will be taken care of." "I will follow up with you tomorrow," instead of "You will be followed up with tomorrow." "I will ensure that this issue is resolved," instead of "This issue needs to be resolved."

TRUST-INDUCING LANGUAGE TYPE	IMPACT	EXAMPLE
Empathetic language	Use empathetic language to show understanding and support for the listener's perspective or emotions. This can increase trust by demonstrating your willingness to listen and empathize with their needs and experiences.	"I can understand how you might be feeling about this situation," instead of "You shouldn't feel that way." "I understand that this situation has been difficult for you," instead of "It's not my problem." "I can understand how you feel, and I want to help you find a solution," instead of "That's not my problem."
Clear intentions	Communicate your intentions clearly and honestly, without manipulating or concealing information. This helps to build trust by demonstrating your integrity and commitment to the conversation or relationship.	"I want to be transparent with you about our company's plans," instead of "I can't really say what we're doing." "I want to make sure we're on the same page about our goals for this project," instead of "We'll just have to see how it goes."

Just as oxytocin can counteract the negative effects of cortisol and promote feelings of well-being and social connectedness, it of course goes without saying that threats, insults, blame, intense emotions, and negative generalizations or using any words that imply harm or danger can all trigger a feeling of impending danger, activate the fight-or-flight response, and trigger feelings of distrust. Persistent exposure to negative or mistrustful language can cause chronic stress, leading to prolonged elevations of cortisol and adrenaline levels in the body. This can have negative effects on the immune system, cardiovascular system, and brain function over time. Research has also shown that the stress hormone cortisol can impair the ability to form new memories and reduce the ability to regulate emotions. This can lead to difficulty in problem-solving, decision-making, and interpersonal relationships.

I have found that clients are often unsure how to phrase difficult conversations or feedback so I thought it would be helpful to offer some suggestions to modify phrasing. I find it helpful to remind oneself, as challenging as it may be in the moment, that you have great power within you to impact the direction of the conversation and eventual relationship based on your maturity and approach to word choice. It is not easy, but learning to take a step back and pause and then speak will become your leadership superpower. It is in those moments that I have the power to create trust but end up harming the relationship and create distrust. Language that can create distrust often involves vagueness, lack of accountability, manipulation, and deception. Language that is manipulative, deceptive, patronizing, dismissive, condescending, or insincere can create distrust with your communication partners and damage your relationships. It's important to communicate in a clear, honest, and direct manner to build trust and credibility.

TYPE OF STATEMENT	EXAMPLE AND SUGGESTED MODIFICATION
Dismissive language	"That's not important right now," instead of "Let's talk about that later when we have more time."
Blaming language	"It's your fault that this happened," instead of "Let's figure out what we can do to prevent this from happening again."
Concealing language	"I can't disclose that information," instead of "I'm sorry, I'm not able to share that with you at this time."
Overpromising language	"I guarantee that this will work perfectly," instead of "I'm confident that we can make this work, but there may be some challenges we need to address."
Condescending language	"You wouldn't understand," instead of "Let me explain this in simpler terms."
Ambiguous language	"It depends," instead of "Can you give me more information so I can provide a clear answer?"
Inconsistent language	Saying one thing and doing another, instead of keeping your word and following your promises
Defensive language	"I didn't do anything wrong," instead of "I understand your concerns, let's talk about how we can resolve this."
Judgmental language	"You're wrong," instead of "I see things differently, can you explain your perspective?"

TYPE OF STATEMENT	EXAMPLE AND SUGGESTED MODIFICATION
Evasive language	"I don't want to talk about it," instead of "I'm not ready to discuss this yet, can we revisit this conversation later?"
Arrogant language	"I know better than you," instead of "Let's work together and come up with the best solution."

It's important to be mindful of the language you use and avoid using words that may trigger a fight-or-flight response in your audience. Instead, focus on using language that is clear, respectful, and collaborative to promote a positive and productive conversation.

CUE AND RECUE

Knowing how to hook and rehook your listeners is the difference between being a talking head and being a dynamic speaker—between being remembered as knowledgeable but unremarkable and being remembered because you were memorable.

A hook is a powerful, to-the-point, relevant way of grabbing the audience's attention. At the beginning of your speech or presentation, it serves to win your audience over—to hook their attention so they have not only a willingness but an urgent desire to hear the rest. It was well put by advertising executive David Ogilvy (no doubt the inspiration for at least one of the characters on the retro television series *Mad Men*), who said, "When you advertise fire-extinguishers, open with the fire."[53]

If you use a hook every time you open a speech, you will consistently begin on a successful note, because you will be engaging the neurochemistry of your audience.

---

53 Bruna Martinuzzi, "12 Ways to Hook an Audience in 30 Seconds," American Express, October 26, 2021, https://www.americanexpress.com/en-us/business/trends-and-insights/articles/hook-presentation-audience-30-seconds/.

I invite you to remember that when you open any speech or communication opportunity, you are viewed as a blank slate. As you begin speaking, your audience is trying to shut down their personal distractions, becoming attuned to your speaking style, your vocalization tone, your physical messaging, assessing your credibility and determining whether or not to listen to you. You have a few short seconds within which to convince them to do so. Keep this in mind and let it guide how you choose to open and close. Select words that will connect you through the five senses, the human experience, valuable information you will share or how the audience will benefit.

Start with a story. Readers are always drawn in by stories about you or someone else. Why are you telling this story? they wonder. What is this story going to teach us?

Some wording is well-known for enlisting audience member's attention because it invites their participation. Think, for example, about the word imagine. I call it the John Lennon Hook.

- Imagine a world where …
- Imagine a place where …
- Imagine a time when …
- Imagine a family where …

Imagine is a huge, powerful word. However, there are plenty of other phrases shown to secure an audience's attention from the start.

- Did you know …
- What if I told you …
- Can you picture …
- Have you ever heard …
- What would you think if …
- Imagine what it would be like …
- Could you see how …

- How could anyone know that ...

When you make these statements, the audience follows you and can visualize what you're describing. You're not fundamentally changing your message. You are pulling the reader into your message, developing trust and interest in what you are going to say next. You are convincing the audience that they will learn something remarkable from you in a given amount of time and that you are worthy of their attention.

Try to avoid hooks for the sake of hooking. You don't want to promise something you can't deliver, and you don't want to sound as if you're showing off. Just take an existing introductory sentence from a presentation or speech you've written and transform it, using the language in one of the hooks mentioned above. That easily, you can engage your audience so that they're eager to hear the rest of your speech.

At one point in the past, an audience could remain engaged, as long as the speaker had originally enticed them with a great hook, for up to fifteen minutes or so before needing to "recue." That is, to reset the flow and grab the attention of the listeners once again. Today, that figure may be even smaller. John Medina, a biologist who studies how the brain processes information, has found that—given a topic of moderate interest—people will begin to tune out after approximately ten minutes.[54] Although his research doesn't suggest you need to end your presentation after ten minutes, it does indicate the need to recue at that point.

And while this can certainly be viewed as a challenge, it shouldn't necessarily be interpreted as bad news. It's been suggested that our

---

54 John Medina, "Winning the Battle for Students' Attention 10 Minutes at a Time," AMLE, accessed November 8, 2021, https://www.amle.org/winning-the-battle-for-students-attention-10-minutes-at-a-time/.

attention spans aren't shrinking as much as they're evolving to fit ever-changing circumstances.[55]

To help you plan how to recue your audience attention, below is a sample visual presentation planning tool which can be used for any length of presentation. You can adapt the time allocated per section but always remember the need to recue using the strategies shared.

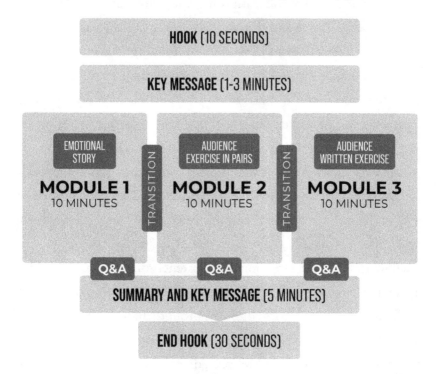

To this point, we have focused a lot on the technical self CQ skills, but I'd like to introduce you to the Audience CQ skills to expand upon the impact you can make.

There is a duality to CQ! It's not just Self CQ, it's also Audience CQ and how you access and influence it.

---

55   Nadjya Ghausi, "Sorry, Goldfish: People's Attention Spans Aren't Shrinking, They're Evolving," Entrepreneur, October 19, 2018, https://www.entrepreneur.c/article/321266.

1. Self CQ: How to adapt yourself, your personal 7/38/55 skills, your mindset.

2. Audience CQ: How to understand whether your audience is receptive and how to maximize their receptivity—specifically discuss neurochemistry of the audience, audience attention, recuing the audience's attention.

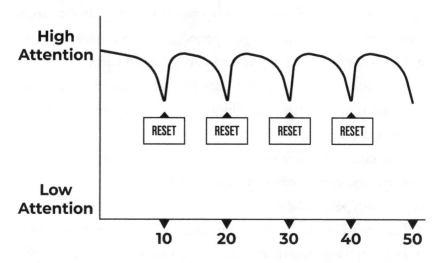

In the art of public speaking, maintaining audience engagement is a dynamic challenge, especially when faced with distractions that can shift your audience's receptivity. To navigate this, you as the speaker must employ various techniques to "rescue" the audience's attention and keep them invested throughout the presentation.

Begin by becoming an astute observer of body language. Signs like restlessness or diverted attention are clear indicators to modify your approach. This could mean altering the tone, the pace, or even the volume of your delivery. Movement across the stage or changing your position can also serve to recapture wandering attention.

Introduce interactive elements like polls, questions, or brief activities. This shift toward participation can rekindle audience interest and break any monotony that may have set in.

If the venue permits, you can try to make strategic use of visual aids to draw eyes back to the front and center as visual stimuli can act as a reset button for wandering minds.

As people are naturally drawn to narratives, weaving relevant stories or examples into your presentation can make complex information more relatable and engaging, thereby regaining lost attention.

I would refer you back to the signposting language in the earlier tables and recommend that you periodically summarize the main points to reinforce your message and bring back the focus.

Pay attention to feedback cues like nods, smiles, or puzzled expressions. These cues can help you adjust your presentation for clarity and engagement.

By mastering these techniques, a speaker can ensure that their message not only reaches the audience but resonates with them, regardless of potential distractions. It's about creating a dynamic interaction, one where the audience remains an active, engaged participant throughout the presentation. Consider this recue diagram to help you plan which strategy you can use to recue at different points in your presentation.

MILLER'S LAW: INFORMATION IN SHORT-TERM MEMORY

To know when you should recue, it is helpful to understand how the brain of your audience processes information.

In the 1950s, a study conducted by George Miller established that short-term memory is limited to seven pieces of information. He created a technique, which became known as Miller's Law, for chunking as a means of grouping information in an effort to extend short-term memory. Later studies included experiments with more pieces of information, but anything beyond seven failed. In the 1980s, chunking[56] was employed again in a study known as the Jacobs Study, in an effort to increase short-term capacity. The study used letters instead of numbers but attained similar findings. The only substantive difference was the realization that numbers were easier to remember than letters. Despite attempts to research since then, no study has conclusively proven that chunking or any other memory technique can go beyond this limit.

HOLD THEIR ATTENTION

When you speak to a group or negotiate a deal or interview for a job, you are essentially asking people to agree with you. To do that, you must first have their attention. Here are some ways to do that.

- Show them something that will fill their needs. If the audience thinks there's something in it for them, you'll find it easier to keep them engaged.
- Point out a threat. We're all afraid of something. One of the messages I try to convey when I speak is what will happen in this race to "beat the bots" if we don't retain and work on the "human" in our human connection of communication.
- Repeat your message using different language and literary devices. Always know your primary message. In the example above, I used "beat the bots." That's powerful for several

---

56 Chunking can improve working memory, which, on average, has a capacity of two to three items. When we change how information is remembered, more input can be stored at a time. For instance, if you are going to the grocery store, you might group similar items together, like fruits and vegetables or packaged goods that can be found in the same store aisle. An added challenge is that most short-term memory is limited to around thirty seconds. This, however, can be extended by repeated verbal repetition. So while chunking itself is more of a hack, this practice, too, is finite and limited.

reasons. First, it's a real concern. Second, the use of the hard letter *b* is strong alliteration and matches the importance of the message. Third, as serious as this concern is, by using the popular slang "bot," the message has a humorous tone. Fourth, it is memorable.

- Use anecdotes. Stories from your own life are especially powerful. "As I was thinking about this meeting today, my daughter came in from school and asked me a question." Stories from the news or from history are also helpful in setting a tone and mood.

- Refer to a historical occasion. Politicians often use this technique. It works because you are tying your current message to something the audience knows really happened. You can do this to contrast your message, to elicit audience fear, or to connect your message with the event and thus validate your position.

- Use a quotation. Although I don't recommend using someone else's words as the first ones out of your mouth, incorporating a humorous or poignant quote will keep your audience involved. It is like a gold nugget you are handing them, one that, if it connects with them, they will keep long after.

- Use humor. Humor is tricky, but when used well, it can engage your audience. Think of humor like salt. You want enough of it to flavor your message, but (unless you are giving a humorous speech) not enough to overwhelm it.

- Ask a rhetorical question. "Who knows?" "Did you hear me?" "Why not?" Ask a rhetorical question for effect, to emphasize your point or your message, when you don't expect an answer.

THE LAST STEP: COMMITTING TO MEMORY

Who said you can't have fun developing your memory? Try some of these techniques and games and feel your brain pulsate.

MIND MAPS AND THE MEMORY TREE

When we were in school, the drill went like this. You read the textbook, you take notes, and you do everything in certain sections. Eventually, you're getting your notes down to one page. That's where the mind map comes in. It is that structure. You remember exactly what comes under each heading for any subject because you know it cold. When you're at that level of mastery in speaking, you can be completely conversational and no longer need to worry about reading from a script.

A mind map is a simple way to visually structure and organize your ideas so that you can recall them at will and maximize your ability to be extemporaneous. Always remember that if you are relying on a script you are unable to fully focus on the 93 percent of your delivery— because you are too busy reading. To reach peak performance I invite you to bear in mind this inversely correlated relationship:

- If your cognitive load is high, your performance will be low: If CL >, then P <.
- If your cognitive load is low, your performance will be high: If CL <, then P >.

The mind map is important for these reasons:
- It bumps up your confidence.
- It improves your memory.
- It removes your dependence on a script.
- It helps you structure ideas.
- It decreases your cognitive load.

189

Mind maps have a central image that represents the key idea. Branches from the central image represent main themes. Each branch has a key word or image on it. Twigs off the branches represent details—ideas that are less central. All parts of the map fit together to reveal the key idea and its details.

You might choose to write out your script in advance. Then create colors as memory reminders. If you know that you want to slow down your pace at a certain part of your speech, use a certain color to indicate that. If you want to emphasize a certain word, maybe use a bright pink. Maybe you want to insert a purposeful pause. Once you highlight a written speech this way and read it many times, you will see those colors when you begin speaking.

The Memory Tree is a simple mind map—as is our burger. It is another way to visualize the structure of your speech. I use the tree to help people expand the content of their presentations.

Let's say your central idea is a new marketing strategy for diabetes medication, and you want to send three main messages about it. Number one, how are you going to help communities? Number two, it's proven to help these communities. And number three, it's going to have huge impact. Then, you could use the tree format. You have your trunk, which is a central idea. And then, you've got your major branches, and your twigs. You could color code each of the twigs as an idea, to show which one to emphasize, and you could highlight particular words within the twigs to emphasize.

Let's simplify it further. If I ask, "What are your plans for the summer?" you can reply randomly, or you can use the tree. Summer is your main trunk. Maybe you have three branches, for June, July, and August. And then, you can add a twig off June and say, "Well, for the first two weeks, I'm going to do this."

People get so many ideas in their minds that they don't know where to place them. But a tree with three branches, main branches, and then twigs that can be color coded is something we can relate to as humans.

All these tools are intended to decrease the cognitive load, which decreases your cortisol level because you have confidence in your memory. Increased confidence equals decreased cortisol and, as we've already discussed, everything is geared toward empowering that lowered fight-or-flight response and that lowered heart rate.

Next, we're going to examine both learning to speak well and with authority, and the importance of using your voice to make an impact. That means paying attention to your tone.

KEY TAKEAWAYS

1. **Hold their attention.** Show your listeners something that fulfills their needs, pointing out a threat, repeating the message using different language and literary devices, using anecdotes, referring to historical occasions, incorporating quotations, using humor, and asking rhetorical questions.

2. **Use mind maps and the memory tree.** Improve memory and enable more fluent and extemporaneous speaking. Mind maps help structure and organize ideas visually, allowing for easier recall. The memory tree is a simplified mind map format that helps expand the content of presentations and speeches.

3. **Decrease your cognitive load.** Reduce your cognitive load to enhance performance. By using techniques like mind maps and the memory tree, individuals can decrease their dependence on scripts, improve confidence, and structure their ideas more effectively. Decreasing cognitive load leads to decreased cortisol levels and increased confidence, which ultimately helps in making a greater impact when speaking.

You have completed the first column of your pre-presentation checklist:

7% CONTENT, STRUCTURE, VOCABULARY, PERSUASION ("WHAT YOU SAY")	38% INTONATION, ARTICULATION ("HOW YOU SAY IT")	55% NONVERBAL COMMUNICATION ("HOW YOU SAY IT")
Speech Burger		
10 hook fish		
PLEK		
Paintbrush		
Persuasive modes		
Speech structures		
Sentence structure or syntax		
Trust-inducing language		
Concise language		
Recueing the audience		
Memory strategies		

CHAPTER 9

Your CQ Checklist—Vocal Impact

Words mean more than what is set down on paper. It takes
the human voice to infuse them with deeper meaning.

—MAYA ANGELOU

If you are to master articulation, elocution, and inflection, you need to grasp upfront how your body works in this regard. We tend to take the way our bodies work for granted and to look at automatic processes as phenomena outside of our control. Physiological functions, however, have an astounding impact on your speaking performance and are well within your control.

Consider the staggering impact of the tongue, cheeks, jaw, lips, and vocal cords when it comes to communication. These parts of your body warrant little attention on a day-to-day basis, but without their harmonious operation, you would not have adequate air—which you need for everything, but especially for projecting your voice and experiencing the sense of calm that precedes confidence. You would not be able to form and enunciate syllables in the words of your planned message.

COLUMN TWO: 38 PERCENT ELEMENTS—TONE, PITCH, ELOCUTION, ARTICULATION, PACE

It is important to remember that we need a key component which is air. This is why there are so many breath exercises as it is essential to how we process, how we deliver our message, how we control our cortisol response. The quality of our voice and its resonance is determined by the air we can access.

7% CONTENT, STRUCTURE, VOCABULARY, PERSUASION ("WHAT YOU SAY")	38% INTONATION, ARTICULATION ("HOW YOU SAY IT")	55% NONVERBAL COMMUNICATION ("HOW YOU SAY IT")

THE PAPER EXPERIMENT

If I were to hand you a piece of paper and say, "Blow on this paper so that it makes noise," what would you do? Some people try to move it, but the easiest way to accomplish the task is to just blow really quickly on the edge of it. Then you will hear the noise of the vibration. This is especially effective as a group exercise. If one person is holding the piece of paper, and everyone is trying to blow on it, nothing will happen, because there isn't enough air aimed in the right direction. When one person takes the paper and blows aggressively on the edge, you have vibration and sound.

The paper is symbolic of your vocal cords. You need to have air passing over them to get sound.

Another way to demonstrate this is with a balloon. Hold a balloon full of air to another person's ear and speak softly from the other side of the balloon. Your voice causes the vibration, a sound wave. The sound wave travels through the air to the balloon, through the balloon to the air inside the balloon, back through the other side of the balloon, through the air again and into your partner's ear. You can hear the sound and feel the vibration through the balloon.[57]

PITCH

Research also shows that deeper voices command more attention than high-pitched ones. In one study, results showed that CEOs with lower voices manage larger companies and, in turn, make more money. Specifically, the analysis found a decrease in voice pitch of 22.1 hertz (Hz) meant an increase in firm size of $440 million, which translated into higher compensation of $187,000 a year.[58]

I'm not saying you should attempt to unnaturally lower your voice. You should, however, be mindful and deepen your voice in times of need or negotiation, where the stakes are higher, and you need to be taken more seriously. The most natural way to do that—and something you can practice before you need it—is to speak from the diaphragm.

This brings to mind some common movie and sitcom characters. Fran Drescher as Fran Fine in *The Nanny* was known for her high-

---

57 "Science Experiment about Sound: Feel the Vibration," Teachers Pay Teachers, accessed January 25, 2022, https://www.teacherspayteachers.com/Product/Science-Experiment-about-Sound-Feel-the-vibration-1636554.

58 Duke University, "New Research Finds There May Be a 'Million Dollar Voice' for CEOs," Fuqua School of Business, April 17, 2013, https://www.fuqua.duke.edu/duke-fuqua-insights/ceo-million-dollar-voice.

pitched and nasally voice, which added to the comedic charm of her character.

Steve Urkel, portrayed by Jaleel White in the TV show *Family Matters*, is known for his unique high-pitched, nasally, and nerdy tone, which became a defining aspect of his character.

Viewers often know immediately upon tuning in that a character who speaks in a nasal voice may exhibit annoying personality traits and will likely rub other characters the wrong way.

Generally, audiences do not respond well to high-pitched voices. If possible, you may consider learning how to lower that pitch. Pitch and pitch control—which is within your ability to train—can have a massive impact on how you are heard.

Contrast the characters noted above with James Earl Jones as the voice of Darth Vader in *Star Wars*, whose deep and commanding voice gave Darth Vader an iconic and distinctive presence. Or consider Morgan Freeman as the narrator in various documentaries and films whose smooth and resonant voice has become synonymous with wisdom and gravitas.

Another voice one can reflect upon is that of Oprah Winfrey. Her voice can be described as warm, rich, and resonant. Her voice possesses a unique blend of clarity, power, and empathy, which has contributed to her success as a renowned media personality and talk show host. Winfrey's vocal delivery is often characterized by a soothing and melodic tone, with a character of authority and confidence. Her voice carries a sense of authenticity and sincerity, capable of commanding attention and connecting with her audience on an emotional level. Overall, Oprah Winfrey's voice is one of her distinctive assets, helping to convey her messages with impact and establishing her as a trusted and influential figure in the world of media and entertainment.

I hope these help bring to light the power of vocal and pitch quality and draw your attention to your current pitch and whether you may want to adapt it for your audience.

The following exercises will help you understand where your voice originates, and they will show you how awareness and exercise together will help you strengthen and control your voice.

HUM BOOT CAMP

The purpose of this exercise is to bring awareness to which parts of your physiology you need to form specific syllables. So for example, if you say the word "Ba," you will note that the burden of forming the syllable falls to your lips. If you say "Ca," you will feel the sound emanating from your throat. And it's possible to get even more specific. For instance, if you say, "Ca ga, ca ga," you will realize that "ca" uses the upper part of your throat, while "ga" calls on the lower part. Learning to pronounce syllables properly is like muscle memory that your body engages on demand when you need it.

VIVALDI

Articulation is key to impact. For the exercise itself, you will say— sing, really—a series of syllables to the first twenty-five seconds of Vivaldi's *The Four Seasons: Spring*. You will do it using consonants, one at a time, with each vowel: bah, bee, bo, bye, cah, cee, co, cye.

This is an articulation exercise spoken to the music (which you can find in the online tracking journal). A lot of people just go *ba, ba, ba, ba*. You need to have the lips touch. If you do this correctly, your mouth will get tired. Try for six syllables a day with a four-day rotation.

TONGUE SWEEP

Your voice is sometimes called the best instrument in the world because you can take it with you wherever you go. Just as you exercise other parts of the body, you have to learn to exercise each part of the body that creates the voice: tongue, teeth, jaw, lips.

Sweep your tongue across your teeth in the following patterns, six times each, ten times a day:

- Sweep from your upper left molar to upper right molar.
- Sweep from your lower right molar to lower left molar.
- Sweep from your lower left molar to lower right molar
- Sweep from your upper right molar to upper left molar.

TONGUE BOOT CAMP

Move your tongue to the front of your teeth and then to the back of your teeth. Then press it against the roof of your mouth and to the back of your throat, as far as you can go. Repeat ten times.

MASAKO MANEUVER

This was originally developed to help those with swallowing disorders. It will also help you. While placing the tip of your tongue between your front teeth, swallow.

THE YAWN

Holding your mouth as wide as possible, yawn for ten seconds.

TONGUE PULL

Stick your tongue as far out as you can. Then pull it in as far back as you can. Hold for two seconds.

CONSCIOUS SWALLOW

Swallow your saliva and at the same time, squeeze your neck and mouth muscles.

GAUZE SWALLOW

Holding a rolled-up cylinder of gauze between your front teeth, bite into it and swallow.

THE GARGLE

Placing your tongue as far back in your throat as you can, pretend to gargle.

TONGUE TWISTER

Press your tongue to the roof of your mouth and say, "Pass the pens and pencils, please," without using your tongue. This exercise will remind you that one needs to have the full physiology engaged to make each particular sound.

Then try to disengage your jaws: open your jaw and try to say those words. You can't do it, can you? Finally hold your breath and try to avoid putting air into those words. It doesn't work. Many people don't realize that breath—air—is so important. This exercise will remind you that you need air to have sound.

THE BUS: ENERGIZE YOUR WORDS!

You want people on that bus with you (i.e., you want your message to reach them), and this tool will help you do that. It's a reminder of the importance of putting emotion into your delivery. Pretend you're a bus driver, and you can affect the people behind you with your voice alone. You can't turn around, and all they see is your back. When you're speaking, the energy you give equals the energy you get.

Here are four sentences. Go ahead and speak them in an almost depressed tone of low energy.

"Are you ready?"

"Are you sure?"

"Are you positive?"

"Let's do it."

Now repeat them, finishing with a verbal question mark at the end—as if you are questioning yourself (lacking confidence).

Now, repeat them again quickly.

Finally, repeat them with lots of energy. Are you ready?

This is a fantastic exercise to prove to yourself that you can generate all this great energy just by changing your tone, articulation, and projection. Automatically, you can feel that you have completely transformed the energy level of people, just with your voice, without access to any nonverbal communication, any facial expressions, even without content—with just four sentences that lack any significant meaning.

To paraphrase a popular quote, people don't always remember what you say, but they remember how you make them feel. And how you make them feel comes not only from the language, but from the tone. If you make them feel energized, they'll remember you. If you make them feel sad, they'll remember that. If you are depressed, and you intend to convey that, fine. Just become mindful and remember the four questions and how tone transformed them.

THE EMOTION WHEEL

Always be aware of both your emotional state and the emotion you wish to convey. If you can identify that emotional state more precisely, through the emotion wheel pictured here—and then inject that emotion into your tone—your result will be powerful.

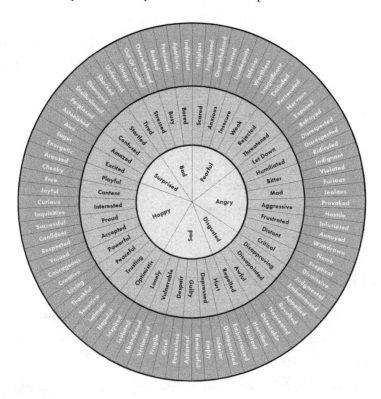

POWER OF PAUSE

Remember the power of the pause. Don't feel that you must fill every moment with speech. Research shows that a purposeful pause automatically engages the audience.[59] So if you want to recue your audience, pausing is an excellent strategy.

---

59   Stefan Benus et al., "Pauses in Deceptive Speech," Columbia University, http://www. cs.columbia.edu/nlp/papers/2006/benus_al_06.pdf.

EMPHASIS

To avoid speaking in a monotone, you need to vary the volume of your voice, and you need to pay attention to emphasis. Audience members are afforded much more information when the speaker adds that emphasis.

For an illustration of just how important it is to consider the stress you place on words, read each of the following, emphasizing the bolded word, and consider what unwritten/unspoken meaning is conveyed by each:

I want a cup of coffee now.

I **want** a cup of coffee now.

I want **a** cup of coffee now.

I want a **cup** of coffee now.

I want a cup **of coffee** now.

I want a cup of coffee **now**.

THE ROLLER COASTER

Are you tone deaf? Would you know if you were? Here's an exercise. Place two fingers in the air as you're speaking and imagine that your voice is on a flat roller coaster moving down the track in a straight line. Say everything in a flat line. Then put your voice higher and change the tone and pace of it, moving your fingers as the roller coaster increases speed and direction. Picture this: put the roller coaster into your voice.

This visual should be your cue to remember that in the nuanced art of communication, the specific focus on tone modulation emerges as a key aspect. Tone modulation refers to the deliberate variation in the pitch and quality of one's voice to enhance communication effectiveness.

Tone modulation will allow you to infuse your speech with emotional subtleties. A softer tone can convey empathy or sincerity, while a firmer tone might express conviction or urgency. This range will help you to accurately convey your emotional intent.

A well-modulated tone can make your arguments more persuasive. For instance, a confident, steady tone suggests authority and can be more convincing, while a varied tone keeps the audience engaged and receptive to the message.

Awareness and development of the right tone can aid in comprehension. A slower, more deliberate tone can be used to emphasize complex points, making them easier to understand, while a lighter, more casual tone can make information seem more accessible.

Very importantly, consistent and appropriate tone modulation can reflect a sense of professionalism and self-assurance. It communicates to your audience that you are competent and confident in your subject matter.

Ride your roller coaster while you remember that tone modulation is your subtle yet powerful tool in effective communication. It will empower you to convey emotions accurately, enhance persuasiveness, aid comprehension, project confidence, adapt to different settings, and maintain audience engagement.

AVERAGE SPEAKING RATE AND WORDS PER MINUTE SKILLS

STOP. TALKING. SO. FAST.

Let us now consider how to layer a third "impact" strategy onto our speech to truly maximally impact our audience; namely, the Pace of Speech. The speed at which you talk greatly influences how the audience perceives you and your speech. We need to understand our speaking rate and how to alter it depending on the speech type we deliver. The average speaking rate changes dramatically for the purpose of your speech. The average conversation rate for English speakers in the United States is about 150 wpm. However, for radio presenters or podcasters, the wpm is higher. This can vary by language and culture but good to consider as a guideline.

Here are a few practical steps to bring awareness to our current pace and how to shift it as required:

1. Adapt our pace of speech based on the environment, the audience, or the context.
2. Think before you speak and adjust pace based on your observations of the audience.
3. Learn how to calculate your speaking rate.
4. Learn how it compares to the average rate for popular talks to give you some context.

As I've mentioned, you need to monitor the rate at which you speak. Fast talkers can give the appearance of trying to talk you into something, like the stereotype of a used-car salesman; so being referred to as a fast talker is less than complimentary. And if having people think you're shady isn't bad enough, talking too fast can also make you appear nervous and uncertain, which you probably are.

English speakers generally speak from 110 to 170 words per minute. What is the best rate? It depends on the situation. A comparison of US presidents' State of the Union addresses from the last several decades puts Ronald Reagan as the fastest speaker, with 116 words per minute, and Donald Trump as the slowest, at 72 words per minute.[60] JFK, who was known as a very fast talker—reaching 327 words per minute in one speech—slowed himself down to 96.5 words

---

60 Emily Atkin, "Trump Is the Slowest Speaker of All Recent US Presidents," New Republic, January 31, 2018, https://newrepublic.com/article/146864/trump-slowest-speaker-recent-us-presidents.

for his inaugural address.[61] For a business presentation, you will want to speak a bit faster: 140 words per minute is recommended.[62]

You can check your speaking speed in any number of ways: online websites like www.speechinminutes.com will translate the number of words in a speech into the duration to read at various speeds. And there are many others. You may even choose to set a metronome at different speeds to get the feel for what each speed is like.

Here's an exercise recommended by a vocal coach to help you take time while you speak:[63]

Choose a paragraph and go through it, inserting slashes to subdivide it into the shortest phrases you can find. Practice reading it like that. If you tend to rush your words under pressure, you might choose to do this daily, using a different paragraph each time. Breathe in and out, paying attention to your abdomen, which should be moving.

Don't be stingy with your air; use it up for each phrase. Think about opening your throat and relaxing your lips, teeth, tongue, and vocal cords. Whisper each phrase. Take your time, pausing between phrases. Repeat the exercise using a normal tone of voice. Keep the air flowing strongly and speak slowly.

Notice how your lips and tongue form the sounds. Bring your awareness to them.

In your ambition to exude a sense of authority, are you sometimes allowing yourself to sound arrogant rather than humble and open? The audience you're speaking to should impact your choice of language. Are you employing a vocabulary level that demonstrates both respect

---

61 https://speakerhubhq.medium.com/
    your-speech-pace-guide-to-speeding-and-slowing-down-be150dcb9cd7.

62 "Speaking Rate," Baruch College, https://tfcs.baruch.cuny.edu/speaking-rate/.

63 This exercise is based on Sims Wyeth's "Fast Talkers: How to Slow Down in Front of
    an Audience," Inc., https://www.inc.com/sims-wyeth/how-to-slow-down-if-you-talk-
    too-fast.html.

for your audience's intelligence and a desire to connect with them (rather than show off to them)?

These are only a few of the considerations that can stem from thinking about how to create a strong vocal image by speaking with authority. Regardless of which principle you're focusing on for your own needs, you can brainstorm a whole list of factors that will help you master it.

Let us turn our minds to how to "impact" and layer the skill of pace over emphasis and articulation. Your mastery of speech pacing will emerge as a pivotal element. It's not just about what you say, but how quickly or slowly you say it. The pace of your speech will have a profound impact on how your message is received and understood—turning your mind toward your Audience CQ.

A key function of speech pace is to aid comprehension and so speaking slowly will be beneficial to you when explaining complex ideas, as it gives the audience time to process the information. On the other hand, a faster pace help you convey excitement and keep the audience engaged with less critical content.

One point which many clients are unaware of is that the speed at which one speaks can mirror your emotional state; this in turn can add a layer of authenticity to your communication. Rapid speech can express excitement or urgency, while a slower pace might indicate seriousness or contemplation.

If you are tasked with a persuasive speech, a balanced speech pace is key to persuasion. Speaking too fast may be perceived as nervousness or lack of preparation, whereas too slow can seem uninteresting. Finding the right pace for your content and audience can significantly enhance your persuasiveness.

In essence, mastering the pace of your speech is not merely a communication technique; it is a critical aspect of impactful and effective communication. It enhances comprehension, engagement, emotional expression, persuasiveness, and authority, making your message not only heard but also felt and remembered. Here are some focus targets that will help you with this skill:

FOCUS TARGET #1	Adapt our pace of speech based on the environment, the audience, or the context.
FOCUS TARGET #2	Think before you speak and adjust pace based on your observations of the audience.
FOCUS TARGET #3	Understand the speaking rate.
FOCUS TARGET #4	Insert a purposeful pause to create a greater effect and recue the audience's attention.
GOAL 1	How to calculate your speaking rate.
GOAL 2	Learn how it compares to the average rate for popular talks to give you some context.
GOAL 3	Exercises to help you develop an adaptive speaking rate.

The speed at which you talk greatly influences how the audience perceives you and your speech. We need to understand our speaking rate and how to alter it, depending on the speech type we deliver. The average speaking rate changes dramatically for the purpose of your speech.

SPEECH RATE GUIDELINES

Slow: less than 110 wpm

Conversational: between 120 wpm and 150 wpm

Fast: more than 160 wpm

Radio hosts and podcasters speak at 150 to 160 wpm.

Auctioneers and commentators speak between 250 and 400 wpm.

To measure your own speech, record yourself speaking for one minute. Convert your speech to text to check the word count. You might be surprised. Many of my clients are.

Do you know how fast or slowly you speak? You can find out with a metronome! As mentioned in an earlier chapter, John F. Kennedy was able to change his speaking pace dramatically. He understood how pacing could change a speech's impact on listeners, and he made good use of this tool.[64]

Also, concentrate on phrasing. Picture the sentence as a unit made up of separate parts, not one big rush of words. You can also think about the punctuation in a sentence. A comma usually means you should slow down.

Once you have control of your pace, you need to consider your message. Martin Luther King's "I Have a Dream" speech would not be delivered in the same pace panelists use to critique performers on *American Idol*.

THE UM POLICE

Maybe you use "um" to punctuate your speeches. Maybe you say "like," "basically," or other filler words. Fillers exist in all languages whether it is "ya'ni" in Arabic, "matlab" in Hindi, "tipo" in Italian, "alors" in French; the list goes on! This is your brain's way of queuing and trying to access information, which is fine. You just don't need to fill in the momentary silence with an unnecessary word. Just pause, bite your tongue or your lip, and stop talking. Fillers contribute nothing, and once you are aware of how many you use, you'll begin to recognize and avoid them.

---

64 "Your Speech Pace: Guide to Speeding and Slowing Down," SpeakerHub, January 22, 2017, https://medium.com/@speakerhubHQ/your-speech-pace-guide-to-speeding-and-slowing-down-be150dcb9cd7.

Give yourself a date, a time, and a topic. Maybe you are going to talk about coffee for thirty seconds. Put a timer on, start recording, begin talking, and then listen to the recording and try to count how many times you used fillers. Listen carefully. One of my clients thought he heard fourteen fillers in two-and-one-half minutes. I counted twenty-seven.

Remember, fillers are very personal, and when you are listening to others, you will start to track their specific fillers, and yours as well.

Here's an exercise for two or more people. The goal is to get the fewest number of points—to use the fewest filler words.

One person picks a random word and is the timekeeper. One person is the speaker. The speaker gets three chances to speak: first for thirty seconds, then forty-five seconds, and finally one minute. Your topics should become increasingly more difficult.

The person who's giving you the topic starts the timer and puts their hands under the table (as does anyone else if there are more than two in this exercise). As soon as they do this, you commence speaking on the topic, using the burger formula. That is, you're using a hook, three points, and an end hook. This is a starter, level one, and as you speak, the person or people with their hands under the table are quietly counting your filler words.

If repeating the topic word is not purposeful, those keeping track should count each repetition as a filler. So if your word is *coffee*, and you say, "Coffee is … coffee is … coffee is … coffee is," you have four strikes without uttering a single "umm."

The people counting don't interrupt the person who is *umm*ing. After each round, they bring up their hands and say something like, "You had four fillers."

Then, one listener tells you what fillers you used, and you write them down. Over time, you will notice that your fillers dissipate, and then they completely disappear. Learning what your fillers are is fascinating. If you just breathe and allow your cortisol to dissipate and decrease, you can simply pause instead. A purposeful pause is more powerful than an unnecessary filler.

The exercise benefits everyone who participates, even the time-keepers. If you do the exercise with a group of three or more, you may notice someone will have heard four fillers, and someone else may have heard three. Someone else will have heard eight. When you realize that you didn't hear as many as others, you know you need to listen more carefully.

Beware of the 14–17 glitch. After going through this exercise with thousands of people, I can say with certainty (and fascination) that the large majority of people tend to blank at fourteen to seventeen seconds. At that point, something happens in the brain or the loop, where you try to access information, and instead, you freeze. If you can get past that—and the burger formula will help you do so—and then learn to expand it through larger burgers and the tree, you will create a structure to get past the 14–17 glitch and keep your train of thought.

So now you know how to grab your audience's attention. You know the importance of tone. As important as these elements are, they will mean little if your gestures and your expressions don't communicate your message.

Finally, we're going to take an in-depth look at nonverbal communication.

KEY TAKEAWAYS

1. **Your pace of speech is pivotal.** Understanding your speaking rate and how to alter it depending on the context is crucial.

Tools like metronome apps and mindful phrasing can help in controlling the pace.

2. **Drop filler words and use silence instead.** Filler words such as "um," "like," "basically," etc., while natural to an extent, should be minimized. Instead of fillers, consider purposeful pauses, which can be more impactful.

3. **Overcome the 14–17 glitch.** Using structures like the "burger formula" or the "tree," speakers can overcome the glitch, ensuring smoother and more coherent speeches.

7% CONTENT, STRUCTURE, VOCABULARY, PERSUASION ("WHAT YOU SAY")	38% INTONATION, ARTICULATION ("HOW YOU SAY IT")	55% NONVERBAL COMMUNICATION ("HOW YOU SAY IT")
	Pitch is key. Bring awareness to your vocal physiology to improve your articulation.	
	Remove fillers.	
	Train your vocal quality through exercises provided.	
	Emphasis: Pause and emotion in your tone are key.	
	Learn to monitor and adapt your pace.	

CHAPTER 10

Your CQ Checklist—Nonverbal Communication

Non-verbal communication is an elaborate secret code that is written nowhere, known by none, and understood by all.

—EDWARD SAPIR

Nonverbal communication goes beyond what we typically think of as body language.

Many *body language experts and sources* seem to agree that between 50 and 80 percent of all human communications are nonverbal.[65] So while the statistics vary according to the situation, it is generally accepted that nonverbal communications are very important in how we understand each other (or fail to), especially in face-to-face and one-to-one communications, and most definitely when the communications involve an emotional or attitudinal element. It is important to keep in mind, unlike spoken words, the transmission

---

65   University of Texas, "How Much of Communication Is Non-Verbal?," The University of Texas Permian Basin, May 15, 2023, https://online.utpb.edu/about-us/articles/communication/how-much-of-communication-is-non-verbal/.

and interpretation can be quite different to the spoken words! Words alone—especially emotional words (or words used in emotional situations)—rarely reflect full or true meaning and motive. One's internal physical state affects observable body language and vocalization, tone, and pitch.

My clients often feel overwhelmed when we start this module because, as you will learn, nonverbal communication is multifaceted. I want to assure you that you've done a lot of the heavy lifting already in chapter 6 when you started controlling your internal cortisol response. Those exercises were purposefully placed early in your tracking journal to help you develop your self-awareness. All that hard work is about to pay off. Nonverbal communication should be authentic. You can learn about what different nonverbal components are, but you will appear robotic if you are fighting fear within your body. As well, if your cognitive load is too high you will be processing to many "to-dos" while trying to present and appear unnatural.

We are programmed within our DNA to judge people subconsciously and to make unconscious assumptions within one-tenth of a second regarding whether this other is a friend or foe. It's a survival mechanism. Once you make that reading, your body responds. For instance, when someone smiles at you, don't you smile back? That's the power of nonverbal communication. Some say that there is a phenomenon called "the Power of Eleven," which says that it can take eleven encounters to undo a poor first encounter; it supports the research that opinions are formed within three to seven seconds. Regardless of whether it is eight, eleven, or twenty encounters to overcome a negative first impression, it highlights the fact that instinctual assessment is often formed a strong view about a new person before they speak a single word. This leads us to consider some interesting facts about why the mastery of nonverbal communications is powerful:

1. Body language enables better self-awareness and self-control.

2. When one understands nonverbal communication one can become better able to refine and improve what our body says about us.

3. This generates a positive improvement in the way we feel, the way we perform, and what we achieve.

4. This enables us to understand more about our own and other people's feelings and meanings.

5. Our reactions to other people's eyes—movement, focus, expression, etc.—and their reactions to our eyes contribute greatly to mutual assessment and understanding, consciously and unconsciously.

6. With no words at all, feelings can be conveyed in a single glance.

So what does this mean for our presentation preparation? How can we use this research to benefit our delivery?

BUILDING AWARENESS

Importantly, understanding body language enables better self-awareness and self-control too. When we understand nonverbal communication, we become better able to refine and improve what our body says about us, which generates a positive improvement in the way we feel, the way we perform, and what we achieve. Nonverbal communication is so important because it can have a significant impact on how we understand each other (or fail to). They can exacerbate or diminish communications that involve an emotional or attitudinal context. Most important, it impacts our memorability factor and can develop (or detract from) the extent to which we are trusted by our audience.

The way to nurture our awareness is to consistently do a "head-to-toe assessment," which I will describe in more detail below. As you may now gather, when I ask you to assess, I would like you to be *micro* in your self-analysis and focus on two prongs for our nonverbal communication—body language which is observable, and body language which is internally impacted.

Observable body language is nonverbal (nonspoken) signals that are exchanged whether these signals are accompanied by spoken words or not. Your own positioning and movements reveal your feelings and meanings to others. Concomitantly, always remember, other people's body language reveals their feelings and meanings to you.

I will not go into the extensive research on how nonverbal communication needs to be adapted based on cultural context but will note that it can make the difference between appearing authentic and being misunderstood. It can bring people together or pull them apart. It can help us speak and read volumes without understanding a word of each other's languages. For example, eye contact, bowing, slouching, hands in pocket, sitting with legs crossed and showing soles of the feet are all viewed differently based on whether you are in the United States, Japan, Turkey, Ghana, or India. Although some of our nonverbal signals appear to be more innate and culturally universal, many others vary considerably among cultures, especially in terms of the use of space (proxemics), eye contact (oculesics), and touch (haptics). Cultural differences cause behavioral and personality differences like body language, gestures, mindsets, communication, manners, and norms, which may lead to miscommunication. This is just something to keep in mind if you are in a diverse organization or traveling for business and presenting for an audience that may need to be adapted for.

Although this chapter focuses on nonverbal communication, I want you to pause for a moment and remind yourself of the importance of communication congruence. That is, each of the nonverbal communication components must align with your vocal variety and the vocabulary and structure of your content. They must all equal and match your intended message, tone, and emotion.

Now that we have some background on the importance of nonverbal communication, let us turn to the specific categories.

COLUMN THREE: 55 PERCENT— NONVERBAL COMMUNICATION

We now move to the third column of our checklist, where we will look at our nonverbal communication.

7% CONTENT, STRUCTURE, VOCABULARY, PERSUASION ("WHAT YOU SAY")	38% INTONATION, ARTICULATION ("HOW YOU SAY IT")	55% NONVERBAL COMMUNICATION ("HOW YOU SAY IT")

PRIMING YOUR BODY FOR AUTHENTIC NONVERBAL COMMUNICATION

As we progress through this key chapter, I invite you to remember four words: your body never lies.

Our body can tell others what we are feeling without us having to say a word. This can be good or, as it is for many, really detrimental to our interactions, presentations, meetings, interviews or in social settings. Before we dive into learning about the vast nonverbal messages that our body communicates, I would ask you to remember that your body will communicate its nervousness if you are unable to control your internal cortisol response. Bearing in mind that nonverbal communication comprises 55 percent of our message, it is important to focus on how to control our inner response to nervousness and then our outward messaging by our gestures, eyes, body.

In addition to the exercises above in chapter 6 to train our vagus nerve and control our beats per minute, you can now add two poses that help to prime your body for success through decreased cortisol and a path to authentic body language. We can train our body to reduce cortisol within through such poses. Hold each of the following for one minute each:

1. Arms up, legs apart.
2. Wrists on hips, elbows bent like a superman, legs apart.

You'll be amazed at how this will transform your ability to control your internal state!

Have you ever noticed that our arms automatically go up instinctively when we rejoice?[66] No one has ever trained an athlete to throw their arms up in happiness when they cross the finish line. Have you ever wondered why they do it? This signifies elation and triumph, as well as initiating a dopamine release.

---

66 "Raise Your Hands In The Air!," Feel Better Do Good, https://www.feelbetterdogood. org/this-week/raise-your-hands-in-the-air.

THE HEAD-TO-TOE ASSESSMENT

Many people assess themselves after they've made a presentation. That's fine. However, remember that when you speak, the audience will be assessing you, and so you need to be self-aware—in the moment. A little secret I would like to share with you is that the more specific you can be on which element of body language you control, the more impactful you will be.

The personal assessment is crucial because you would otherwise skip over something you're not even aware you're doing. As we turn to this third column of our CQ Pre-Presentation Checklist, I will ask you to be very specific about which category of nonverbal communication you are focusing on. It is not enough to say, "general" body language, as most will refer to it!

To be specific, please do a head-to-toe assessment of the different elements of your body to bring awareness to the many categories of nonverbal communication.

A quick and easy way to do this is to take a smartphone video of yourself as you are speaking!

The sending and receiving of signals happen on conscious and unconscious levels, the unconscious and conscious transmission and interpretation of feelings, attitudes, and moods, through:

1. Forehead
2. Eyebrows
3. Oculesics: Eyes and direction of eye movement
4. Mouth
5. Chin
6. Cheeks
7. Neck
8. Shoulders

9. Arm gesticulation
10. Hand gesticulation
11. Finger gesticulation
12. Leg positioning
13. Feet placement and direction
14. Position and relationship to other bodies, objects, and surroundings
15. Facial expressions combining each of the above
16. Posture
17. Proxemics (five zones of personal space)
18. Mirroring and matching of body signals
19. Haptics—touch
20. Dress

You can use these parts of your body as a guide to drawing your attention to how *you* present physically. The way to bring awareness includes specificity such as this:

- Starting with the location of the tip of your head, scan down to your forehead, and consider if you are furrowing your brow. Stop and ask yourself, "Why am I furrowing and what message am I relaying to the audience?"
- Next, move to your eyes, and assess what direction your eyes are looking. Or, you may observe for example that, perhaps, one eye is twitching.
- Next, consider the direction of the tilt of your head.
- Continuing downward, consider your lips and whether they are pursed, tight, or smiling genuinely. If they are pursed, consider why. Has something in the environment triggered you to be fearful or angry?

Continue downward …

Although we do not have space to cover all these twenty components, we will focus on some key ones which I have grouped into five categories. This will guide you to become more specific in assessing your personal nonverbal communication and shifting your mindset and inner voice in the moment. Here's what you should concentrate on:

1. Facial expressions
2. Eye contact
3. Posture
4. Gesticulation—hands and arms
5. Legs and feet

As we progress through these five categories, I invite you to create a bespoke checklist of how each of the elements of nonverbal communication present within you. You can use this in the future to self-assess before and after a presentation and see how you grew. You can start noting these into your Tracking Journal as we progress through each category of nonverbal communication.

Next, let's turn to each of the five categories:

FACIAL EXPRESSIONS

Yes, you can be aware of your facial expressions, and doing so when you speak is essential. We can't change our appearance, but we can overcome any character signals inherent to our genetic facial structure by modifying our expressions. If you do a head-to-toe assessment of yourself, you'll realize what micromessages you're sending through something as simple as the twitch of a cheek or a flicker or change in gaze.

A 2014 scientific study found that in less than the blink of an eye, people make unconscious assessments of others.[67] Researchers in this study monitored the amygdala (emotional center of the brain) of participants who were presented with pictures of human faces. In a mere thirty-three milliseconds, participants in the study indicated whether they trusted the face (and the person behind it)—a period so short it excluded conscious insight. The study details factors such as facial structure, expression, eyes, etc. that influence our assessment of them.[68]

Did you know that people in the United States use the same facial expression for sadness as indigenous people in Papua New Guinea who have never seen TV or movies do? That people who were born blind use the same facial expressions as well? Dr. Paul Ekman of the University of California at San Francisco created the facial action coding system (FACS). His research points out seven universal emotional expressions: sadness, happiness, anger, interest, fear, contempt, and surprise.

Mirror exercises are especially helpful in learning how you express these emotions. Don't overdo them, or you will look like a caricature. Ask yourself whether your facial expressions match your words. Most of all, be yourself. These exercises work best when you learn how to express your feelings through your facial expressions.

Have you ever had a moment where you are trying to project pure confidence at an event or during a speech and you can feel your cheeks quivering or part of your upper lip quivering uncontrollably?

67   Jonathan B. Freeman et al., "Amygdala Responsivity to High-Level Social Informa-tion from Unseen Faces," *Journal of Neuroscience 34*, no. 32, 10573–10581, https://static1.squarespace.com/static/5daf65330e17a4220c7707ce/t/5dbf8ffd52537379a682e021/1572835327205/amygdala-responsivity-to-high-level-social-information-from-unseen-faces.pdf.

68   Joseph Guarino, "Know Your Resting Face," Institute of Public Speaking, January 17, 2022, https://www.instituteofpublicspeaking.com/body-language/know-resting-face.

Your body is literally fighting itself in such situations; it is not you—it happens to people around the world. Authenticity is key to delete such expressions. This can be achieved by reducing your cognitive load. Let us learn how in relation to your facial expressions and gesticulation and body language.

Just as others read you, you also read them, although it isn't as easy to read people as it was in the days before cosmetic fillers and surgery. I'm sure you've seen the telltale signs of cosmetic fillers—a certain waxy quality to the forehead. Botox and other fillers paralyze facial muscles and minimize microexpressions that reveal fleeting glimpses of unconscious feelings. Just as important, fillers limit your ability to mimic the facial expressions of others, which is critical in the formation of empathy.

"While primates also engage in facial mimicry, evolution gave humans the advantage of more refined musculature, especially around the eyes, and we have thinner and smoother skin, making it easier to see the tiniest twitches," says a *New York Times* article.[69] The result is that humans have a greater number of facial expressions—thousands, in fact—that we detect with amazing speed and precision. This ability to read one another and empathize has arguably been fundamental to all human achievement. "Facial mimicry is a very ancient mechanism of connecting and not something you want disrupted by Botox or other procedures," said Frans de Waal, a primatologist and ethologist at Emory University. "Today I think primates are sometimes more perceptive than humans at reading facial expressions and body

---

69   Kate Murphy, "Changing Your Lips May Change You," *New York Times*, April 23, 2019, https://link.gale.com/apps/doc/A583223429/SPJ.SP24?u=ntn&sid=bookmark-SPJ. SP24&xid=5cc79043.

language because that's all they have to go by, whereas we are always waiting for the words—and words can be highly misleading."[70]

SMILES

Named after the French physician Guillaume Duchenne, who studied the physiology of facial expressions in the nineteenth century, the Duchenne smile involves both voluntary and involuntary contraction from the zygomatic major (the muscle raising the corners of the mouth) and the orbicularis oculi (the muscle raising the cheeks and producing crow's feet around the eyes). Compare this to the fake smile that contracts only the zygomatic major. The two smiles are controlled by different parts of the brain.

When a patient with damage to the motor cortex on the brain's left hemisphere attempts to smile, the smile is asymmetrical, with the right side not moving as it should. However, when that same patient spontaneously laughs, the smile is normal! This means that the genuine smile is controlled by some other part of the brain. When a patient with damage to the anterior cingulate (part of the limbic system) in the left hemisphere attempts to smile, the smile is normal. However, when that same patient smiles spontaneously, the asymmetry appears.[71]

The fake smile is controlled by the motor cortex, and emotion-related movements, including the Duchenne smile, are controlled by the limbic system, which is the emotional center of the brain. The contraction of the muscles surrounding our eyes is extremely difficult to do voluntarily and therefore is a good indicator of true enjoyment.

---

70   Kate Murphy, "Can Botox and Cosmetic Surgery Chill Our Relationships With Others?," *New York Times*, April 26, 2019, https://www.nytimes.com/2019/04/18/well/mind/can-botox-and-cosmetic-surgery-chill-our-relationships-with-others.html.

71   Adoree Durayappah-Harrison, "What Science Has to Say About Genuine vs. Fake Smiles," Psychology Today, January 5, 2010, https://www.psychologytoday.com/us/blog/thriving101/201001/what-science-has-say-about-genuine-vs-fake-smiles.

An easy way to spot the difference is to look for wrinkling around the outside of the eye. If these wrinkles appear or become deeper, it is likely the orbicularis oculi is engaged, and you are witnessing a "genuine smile."[72] A pasted smile is one that appears quickly, is fixed for longer than a natural smile, and seems not to extend to the eyes. This typically indicates suppressed displeasure or forced agreement of some sort.

A tight-lipped smile is stretched across the face in a straight line, teeth concealed. The smiler has a secret they are not going to share, possibly due to dislike or distrust or can also be a rejection signal or show fear or the masking of one's true emotions. If the lips are pulled inward, it can mean the person is "holding in" words and emotions. Conversely, what I call the "Marilyn Monroe smile," the open mouth smile, almost as if the lips have been frozen while laughing, is not genuine either, yet it conveys playfulness. What I refer to as the "Princess Diana smile," where one lowers the head and looks slightly away and up while smiling, makes you appear shy and vulnerable.

Try each of these smiles and see what you think!

Although smiles show our joy, our openness, and even our vulnerability, they are also tools used by those who wish to take advantage of us. The practiced smile where the jaw is dropped lower than a natural smile of the salesperson, regardless of whether that person is selling a car, a political ideology, or even a religion, has a sameness to it, as if the speaker has put it on along with whatever clothing he or she is wearing. Once you've seen a few of these, you'll know them for what they are. Avoid them in your own communication.

---

72 "The Discovery of the Duchenne (Genuine) Smile," Paul Ekman International, accessed January 17, 2022, https://www.ekmaninternational.com/wiki/the-duchenne-smile/.

When speaking, let your emotions guide when you smile. If you care about something, and a smile feels natural, don't hold it back. When it is a genuine response, it will elicit a positive response from your audience.

LIPS

If we get more specific and consider just the lips, when one has pursed lips, it is as if one is holding the words in the mouth until they are ready to be released. This can also indicate anxiousness or impatience at not being able to speak. Or quite differently can indicate upset, as if suppressing crying. Alternately, biting one's lips might signal tension or stress or anxiety.

EYE CONTACT

Let's suppose you and I are speaking in person, and we make eye contact. That simple action causes our brains to release certain chemicals based on how it is culturally perceived. For example, eye contact in some parts of Asia would be considered rude, thus inducing a feeling of defiance, lack of trust, or lack of respect.

Compare this with Western culture, where lack of eye contact might be perceived as though one is lying, mistrustful, awkward, shy, "tuned out," disinterested, or anxious. Yet it's hard for humans to process vocabulary, recall which words to use, place them in the "appropriate" order and tone, all while looking directly in someone's eyes. It is called cogitating when a human breaks eye contact so they can process what information is being received/shared—imagine that emoji on your phone where it appears like a head explodes. That is actually what it feels like for some when they try to hold another's gaze while speaking. For those who "cogitate" one strategy might be to use other nonverbal communication strategies outlined below to help cope and "buy some time" through nonverbal distraction. In

Western societies, one should aim to maximize eye contact with the following in mind.

Various chemicals are released when we interact with each other. They include oxytocin, dopamine, serotonin, cortisol, and endorphins. Which chemical is released is what determines how engaged and connected we are to the conversation. In the event that our interaction induces trust, we increase oxytocin, a bonding hormone (sometimes called the love hormone). So we physically impact each other when we speak, even though no touch is occurring.

When you connect through eye contact, you increase oxytocin which is known as the bonding/love hormone. Oxytocin is a neuropeptide that plays a crucial role in social bonding, trust, and affection. It is often referred to as the "cuddle hormone" or "love hormone" because its release is associated with feelings of love, trust, and attachment. Oxytocin is produced in the hypothalamus, a region of the brain, and is released into the bloodstream by the pituitary gland.

Interestingly, to understand the power of this hormone for those who have given birth, the release of oxytocin during childbirth and breastfeeding helps establish the bond between a mother and her newborn. It promotes feelings of attachment, nurturing, and the desire to care for and protect the baby. This bonding process is crucial for the emotional and social development of both the mother and the baby.

Now knowing the power of eye contact, we can understand the need to focus on maintaining it by pushing through the awkward feeling it may elicit. To do so, you literally need to speak to yourself in the moment and guide yourself to maintain eye contact. I invite you to add this to your goal list—I promise it will become natural and the odd feelings will dissipate and eventually disappear. Often, maintaining eye contact can be uncomfortable. Still, mastering this skill is essential.

Our ability to engage in eye contact may actually be impacted by how we believe we are perceived by others and the degree of our self-consciousness. Several studies[73] demonstrate that when we feel people are looking at us, this triggers the body's physiological responses (heart rate, sweating, and breathing) as well as concern about how we are being perceived by others.

Additionally, we like people (and animated characters) more when they are looking directly into our eyes—provided the eye contact is offered in a nonthreatening situation.

One study suggests that people are comfortable with eye contact for only 3.2 seconds at a time with strangers.[74] The time extends when they know the other person or when you have higher stakes in engaging the audience. That's when you are addressing someone one-on-one. However, when addressing a group, maintain eye contact with one audience member for at least four seconds before moving to another audience member.

If you want to overcome your discomfort of making extended eye contact with strangers while you're speaking to them, you should alternate your gaze between audience members in different locations of the room.

Direct eye contact can be divided into two categories: while speaking and while listening. Direct eye contact while one is speaking is regarded as a sign of truthfulness. When one engages in direct eye contact while one is listening, it indicates attentiveness,

73   Katherine Schreiber, "What Eye Contact Can Do to You," Psychology Today, September 20, 2016, https://www.psychologytoday.com/us/blog/the-truth-about-exercise-addiction/201609/what-eye-contact-can-do-you.

74   Melinda Wenner Moyer, "Eye Contact: How Long Is Too Long," Scientific American, January 1, 2016, https://www.scientificamerican.com/article/eye-contact-how-long-is-too-long.

interest, and attention. Likewise, widening the eyes can indicate interest or an invitation.

Eyebrows are also a very important part of human expression and communication. They allow us to show our emotions and thereby can aid in reinforcing our message, or make our face appear unintentionally sad or angry. If you add a raised eyebrow it may indicate disapproval, skepticism or surprise, while two raised eyebrows may indicate shock. Secret tip - Well-groomed eyebrows can have great impact on your facial appearance and quality of expressions.

Your blinking rate can also send messages to your audience. An infrequent blink rate, for example, may indicate boredom if the eyes are not focused (i.e., may appear as if one is "zoned out"). Alternately, it may indicate concentration and focus. Infrequent blink rate can also be accompanied by signals of hostility or negativity and is therefore not the most revealing of body language signals. A low blink rate combined with other facial expressions may come across as a glare or anger.

Incorporate full body movement to match your eye contact when appropriate. For example, tilting your head usually means you're engaged, concentrating, and listening intently. A hand to the cheek also shows that you're carefully evaluating what is being said. When someone does this when you are speaking, it usually indicates that they are taking what you are saying seriously.

In the tracking journal, there are some exercises to help you become more comfortable in increasing your eye contact with strangers as I know it is "easier said than done" for most.

GESTICULATION

Gestures are some of your most powerful visual aids because, unlike charts, graphs, or videos, they come spontaneously from you and engage the imaginations of your audience members. Because gestures carry so much emotional weight, be careful not to overdo them so that you don't appear cartoonish or mime-like. As mentioned above, you should start with your hands relaxed on either side of your body.

Hands on your hips can be read two ways. You may appear angry and aggressive, or you may simply appear to be expressing excitement and enthusiasm.

When referring to a visual aid, glance at the screen to engage your audience. Don't turn and face it, and don't read from it. You can gesture to indicate shapes and sizes, or you can lift a number of fingers to emphasize a specific number such as, "Ten times more."

HANDS/PALMS

What always amazes me is the power of messaging that can be shared with one's hands. We have the power to communicate authority, strength, dominance, striving for or seeking an answer, aggression, threat, emphasis, warning, refusal, thoughtfulness, looking for or explaining connections or engagement, thoughtfulness—the list goes on.

Therefore, if we can arm ourselves with the knowledge of what different gestures mean, we empower ourselves to be great communicators.

When considering your hands, take a micro approach and bring awareness to the direction of movement, speed of movement and location of placement, of your palms, back of hand, side of hands, fingers, and fingertips.

For example, will you place your palms upward or downward? Did you know that you send messages of openness and trust based on the direction your palms face? Using an upward facing open hand palm is said to evolve from when open upward palms showed no weapon was held. As a common gesture with various meanings around a main theme of openness, this can also mean "I don't have the answer," or it can be an appeal. In some situations, this can indicate confidence (such as to enable openness), or trust/trustworthiness. Outward open forearms or whole arms are more extreme versions of the signal.

If you place your hand on your heart (on the left side of your chest) this indicates your request to be believed, whether being truthful or not. Hand to heart center is a lovely way to express thanks.

In contrast, where the lower arm moves across the body with palm down this is generally defiance or firm disagreement. If your palms are facing upward and moving up and down as if they're weighing something, the empty hand figuratively holds a problem or idea as if you are weighing it akin to a symbol for weighing possibilities. The side of the hand can be used like a guillotine, as if to kill the discussion.

When trying to express resistance, aggression, determination, hands can be powerful. One or two clenched fists can indicate different feelings—defensive, offensive, positive, or negative, depending on context and other signals. Logically a clenched fist prepares the hand (and mind and body) for battle of one sort or another, but in isolation, the signal is impossible to interpret more precisely than a basic feeling of resolve.

FINGERS

Fingers, like hands, can be key in expressing emotion ranging from aggression, threat, emphasis, acknowledgement, admonishment, refusal, and authority.

Pointing at a person is very confrontational and dictatorial. At times adults would gesture this way to younger people. Adult to adult it is generally unacceptable and tends to indicate a lack of social awareness or self-control, in addition to arrogance on the part of the finger pointer. The finger can also be perceived as representing a gun or a pointed weapon. In other words, it's strongly associated with anger being directed at another person.

An exception to the generally aggressive meaning of finger-pointing is the finger point and wink, below. The subtle use of a winked eye with a pointed finger changes the finger point into a different signal, that of acknowledging something, often a contribution or remark made by someone, in which case the finger and wink are directed at the person concerned, and can be a signal of positive appreciation, as if to say, "You got it," or "You understand it; well done."

When one connects their fingertips and thumbs touching on opposite hands this is called steepling. This gesture reflects complex and/or elevated thinking. In this gesture only the fingertips touch—each finger with the corresponding digit of the other hand, pointing upward like the rafters of a tall church roof. The direction upward-pointing versus forward facing can send different messages of being a defensive or distancing barrier or communicating thoughtfulness.

POSTURE

Posture sets the tone for "body language package" you deliver. When we look at the list of twenty elements above, they combine to convey meaning. The way you stand, walk, and sit are all heavily influencing the way that others perceive you. The way you sit or stand can also communicate your comfort level, professionalism and general disposition toward a person or conversation. It impacts how people view your level of confidence and whether you are trusted.

Straight posture also "says" you are interested in what the other person is saying, and you value the conversation. Slouching indicates a lack of interest in the other person and their words, or that you don't care how they think about you. Poor posture can also indicate a lack of self-esteem.

What happens is when one is nervous, they may lose track of what their body is doing. We can train our body in advance so we go into "autopilot" when presenting. Below are a set of visuals to help remind you how to maximize your posture:

STRING GIRAFFE

Imagine you're a giraffe attached to the ceiling with a piece of string, and if I ask you to tug on the hair at top of your head (or pinch your scalp if you lack hair), and I do this over and over again, you probably won't forget that visual, that physiological tug. Your brain has just registered that you need to remember to connect to the upper part of your body and to elongate your neck to increase your projection. With your chin up and head high, you increase your vocal capacity.

LEGS AND FEET

Leg movement is often overlooked or taken for granted as a nonverbal cue. You may not have thought about it before but in actuality, the legs transmit a wide variety of emotions, where leg position and movement can relay messages ranging from elegance to nervousness to joy.

LEGS WHEN STANDING

Often people stand in a "legs-together position" which messages that their boundaries are up and they are not very open to the person in front of them. If you were to shift and stand legs apart you are conveying that you are more open to the other person in the conversation and feel confident in yourself. This is linked with territory that is claimed by displaying your legs apart and the extent of territorial physical distance placed between two individuals.

When someone feels confident, they might try to make themselves seem taller by standing up straight with their legs apart and their hands on their hips—this is called the "standing tall" position. From this position, one can move in any of the four directions by bending one leg while keeping the other leg straight. Standing tall will send a clear signal of confidence to others. Others become aware of your presence as you enter a room.

Standing upright, legs straight, together, and parallel, with the body quite upright, shoulders back, arms by sides—this is like the military "at attention" posture and is often a signal of respect or subservience adopted when addressed by someone in authority. The soldier stance is used in very formal situations and is typical for people who are inferior to a more dominant individual. Similarly, a territorial stance is when one person stands with their arms crossed, leaning back legs spread apart. This stance can be seen as a defensive and aggressive one and may be used to intimidate the person they're talking to and also sends a signal of confidence and subconsciously claims territory.

Where legs are crossed and arms are not, this can indicate a submissive or committed agreement to stand and engage, so the standing leg cross relays potentially quite different things. If you are standing with your legs crossed, it may indicate insecurity or being defensive. The final determination of the message could be impacted, for example, by the other body parts such as where legs are crossed and arms are not; this can indicate a submissive or committed agreement to stand and engage.

As well, I would ask you to be specific in considering which angle and side you stand relative to another person can give off different meanings and can change the extent to which we are seen as a threat. If we stand in front of them, it could send the signal that we are challenging them for a fight. This will trigger their internal defense process, whether they are fighting or fleeing.

As a final note, it's important to consider at which angle and on which side you stand relative to another person. This can give off different meanings and can change the extent to which we are perceived as a threat. The way we stand in front of someone could send the signal that we are challenging them. This may trigger an internal defense process and decrease audience trust.

LEGS/FEET WHEN SEATED

Often, meetings are seated. Do not miss the opportunity to amplify your message using these tools or consider how to modify your seated posture in different environments.

In sitting positions, one's leg direction can signal unintended meanings and messages. It is notable that these may be impacted by gender and cultural programming but nonetheless can impact how one is perceived.

For example, open uncrossed leg positions generally indicate an open attitude, contrasting with crossed legs, which normally indicate a closed attitude or a degree of caution or uncertainty. Generally, a seated person directs their knee or knees toward the point of interest. The converse is true also—legs tend to point away from something or someone which is uninteresting or threatening. Splayed legs, that is wide-parted legs create (usually unconsciously) a firm base from which to defend or attack, and also make the body look wider and would, for example, be supported if hands were on one's hips.

The rule applies with crossed legs also, where the upper knee indicates interest or disinterest according to where it points. The more direct and obvious the position, the keener the attraction or repellent feeling. Historically, in some cultures, if the knees point at an angle rather than straight ahead, this posture was common in women due to upbringing and clothing and indicates a sense of properness. When legs are crossed, generally, the upper crossed leg and knee will point according to the person's interest. If the knee points toward a person then it signifies interest in or enthusiasm for that person—if it points away from a person it signifies disinterest in or a perceived threat from that person. Signs are more indicative when people first sit down and adopt initial positions in relation to others present. Signs become less reliable when people have been sitting for half an hour or so, when leg crossing can change more for comfort than body language reasons. When one sits ankle locked, there can be a messaging of defensiveness, whether knees are apart (among men predominantly) or together (more natural in women) and there may also be a suggestion of suppressing negative emotions.

FEET

Like knees, feet tend to point toward the focus of interest—or away from something or someone if it is not of interest. Foot direction or pointing in this context is a subtle aspect of posture—this is not using the foot to point at something; it is merely the direction of the feet when sitting or standing in relation to people close by. When one places their foot forward, the signal is interesting among groups when it can indicate perceptions of leadership or dominance (i.e., the forward foot points at the leader or strongest member of the group).

Feet can tell you a great deal about someone, and they can tell others a great deal about you. If you shuffle your feet, it could tell others that you want to leave the situation, that you are uncomfortable or nervous. If you are walking with others, do so briskly and with confidence.

There are many other minutiae of leg and foot positioning, but this gives you a sense of how to analyze your body.

PIZZA SLICE

This is a reminder of where your feet should be if standing. Legs should be hip width apart. Pointed forward is best. Pointed out, ballerina style, is awkward, and pointed in signals lack of confidence. Imagine the space between your legs as about the shape of a slice of pizza. You can always remember how a pizza slice looks, regardless of how tense the situation around you may be!

BODY LANGUAGE IN THE VIRTUAL AND ONLINE WORLD

A final note before we dig deeper into this fascinating topic of virtual body language. It was noted above that we need to adapt our communication in online environments. Face-to-face interactions are predominantly synchronous, meaning they occur naturally. Each listener has instantaneous receipt and a quick response. Online communication can also be synchronous with rapid-fire responses, but it can also be asynchronous when viewing a recording. Nonverbal communication adds nuance or richness of meaning that cannot be communicated by verbal elements alone, but this can often be lost in online settings and therefore needs to be compensated for through our vocal variety and content.

Here's a checklist to prepare for online communication:

- **Use facial expressions.** You will need to compensate for the lost nonverbal opportunities through mindful facial expressions.
- **Play with tone and vocal variety.** You will need to share your energy and enthusiasm through your shift of tone, purposeful pause. Refer back to the chapter on Vocal Variety and practice these!

- **Camera setup is key.** Your camera should be at eye level, so that your gaze appears natural to others. Think of centering yourself in the screen like a newscaster.
- **Lighting.** It should be well-lit with no shadows.
- **Background.** Keep this simple. A blank wall or virtual background can be best.
- **Maintain eye contact.** Look into the camera as if you're looking into the person's eyes, or look around at the participants in a group call to show engagement.

DON'T LEAVE IT TO CHANCE

When you practice nonverbal cues, you convince not only your audience but yourself. My message in this chapter is: *don't leave your body language to chance.* You don't have to memorize every gesture or panic if you find you've just crossed your arms when you meant to gesture with your palms up. But if you are aware of these basic gestures, expressions, and postures, you will be able to convey what you actually mean. That's why nonverbal communication is so important, so that you can communicate your message to your audience in the most impactful way. Remember that you also need to remember what *not* to do—which cues send messages of mistrust or lack of confidence. Use the lists provided to bring awareness to your body and the messages you emit. Messages equal chemical balance. Remember this to help you control and *mindfully move to match your message.*

As you practice, you will become more authentic in your presentations. Even if you have felt awkward, shy, or nervous in the past, these tools will become more and more natural as you use them—because they are. In order to get the most from them, you may need to put aside some of the beliefs you've previously had about yourself and your ability to communicate. We're going to look at them in the next chapter.

KEY TAKEAWAYS

1. **Build awareness of your facial expressions.** These play a significant role in nonverbal communication and influence how others perceive us. By being aware of our facial expressions, we can modify and control the micro messages we send.

2. **Work with the Duchenne smile.** It's characterized by the contraction of muscles around the mouth and eyes, is a genuine and natural smile that indicates true enjoyment.

3. **Use eye contact skillfully.** Your eyes create a powerful form of nonverbal communication that affects how we are perceived and can elicit physiological responses. Maintaining eye contact shows attentiveness, interest, and truthfulness. However, the comfort level with eye contact varies, and different cultural contexts should be considered.

7% CONTENT, STRUCTURE, VOCABULARY, PERSUASION ("WHAT YOU SAY")	38% INTONATION, ARTICULATION ("HOW YOU SAY IT")	55% NONVERBAL COMMUNICATION ("HOW YOU SAY IT")
		Minimize your cortisol response to increase confidence in body language
		Conduct a head to toe assessment of your baseline non-verbal communication messaging
		Check and adapt each element of your body based on your audience while maintaining your controlled heart rate
		Face, lips Eyes, eyebrows Gesticulation, hands, palms, fingers, Posture, Legs, feet Adapt for the online world

CHAPTER 11

Next Step—Find Your Safe Place

*I've been absolutely terrified every moment of my life—and I've
never let it keep me from doing a single thing I wanted to do.*

—GEORGIA O'KEEFFE

When I work with a client, I always tell that person that this is a safe
place, your sanctuary. Everything said and everything that happens
during the course of our work together stays here. People know they
can completely reveal themselves to me while going through the
process of introspection in a nonjudgmental, trusting environment
that allows them to dig deeply and figure out what is really causing
some of their layers of insecurity. Sometimes when you just release
those feelings, you can then parse through them and address the cause.
That's what I want to provide for you in this book and in the six-week
journal that follows.

Although we are not sharing the privacy of a session or a workshop
together, I want you to try to create a safe space here, and I highly
encourage you to keep the private journal at the end of this book in
which you are completely honest with yourself and where you take

time to reflect on past events that might have led you to question your ability to shine to the best of your potential. Be detailed in your reflections, so your goal setting will be detailed as well.

I invite you to create a communication menu that works with your goals and demands of your lifestyle. The key is to make these habits into a routine with a focus on the target micro goal and an understanding of how this fits into your plan for personal transformation. When you can shift your behavior in this way consistently, it changes your personal life. For example, you could consider a routine such as this one:

1. Review your schedule for the week.
2. Determine which meetings are planned for the week.
3. Set which personal goal can be targeted during a specific meeting(s).
4. Create a list of what preparation needs to be completed and by when.
5. Consider if there is a narrative you want to share during that meeting.
6. Determine what vocal image you want to relay during this meeting.
7. Determine what vocabulary will help you achieve that vocal image and achieve your targeted goal.
8. Schedule in specific times when you will practice the exercises.
9. Add in daily time for articulation exercises and breath exercises—give the time calculation—should take only four to five minutes each day as per worksheet.
10. Journal before and after the meeting to track worries, successes, and future targets for improvement.

As a frequent flier on Emirates, there was historically one notable section on their menu that caught my attention. It was the section called "As You Like It." These included treats that are always available to flyers when they are feeling a bit peckish. Likewise, I would like you to schedule in the exercises learned throughout this book and then sprinkle in a few others whenever you are able. This will help you commit to a CQ Ethos in your life and truly commit to your transformation through daily practice. Here is the summary of all the tools by column for your ease of reference. Consider this to be your complete PPCL (Pre-Presentation Checklist) or cheat sheet! (Insert a complete table with all three columns showing all the tools outlined.)

EXECUTION: SPECIFICS AND DETAILS

It is time to put all these strategies into action without feeling overwhelmed. Below is your at-a-glance Pre-Presentation Checklist. This is your quick reference synopsis of all the tools you have acquired in summary format.

7% CONTENT, STRUCTURE, VOCABULARY, PERSUASION ("WHAT YOU SAY")	38% INTONATION, ARTICULATION ("HOW YOU SAY IT")	55% NONVERBAL COMMUNICATION ("HOW YOU SAY IT")
· Speech Burger · 10 Hook Fish · PLEK · Paintbrush · Persuasive Modes · Speech Structures	· Pitch is key. Bring awareness to your vocal physiology to improve your articulation. · Remove fillers. · Train your vocal quality through exercises provided.	· Minimize your cortisol response to increase confidence in body language · Conduct a head to toe assessment of your baseline non-verbal communication messaging

7% CONTENT, STRUCTURE, VOCABULARY, PERSUASION ("WHAT YOU SAY")	38% INTONATION, ARTICULATION ("HOW YOU SAY IT")	55% NONVERBAL COMMUNICATION ("HOW YOU SAY IT")
· Sentence Structure or Syntax · Trust-inducing language · Concise language · Recueing the audience · Memory strategies	· Emphasis: Pause and emotion in your tone are key. · Learn to monitor and adapt your pace.	· Check and adapt each element of your body based on your audience while maintaining your controlled heart rate · Face, lips · Eyes, eyebrows · Gesticulation, hands, palms, fingers, Posture, · Legs, feet · Adapt for the online world

Here's an example of a practical way to implement so you can track progress on a weekly basis. I will start with an everyday life example as it may be easier for some to understand and contrast with how a client would use a similar approach in a business context.

If one of our four daughters goes to a golf lesson, she will come home thinking about what she learned from that experience, and at our weekly family meeting that Saturday evening, she might analyze her swing and set a goal about how she is going to improve it. We don't speak in generalities. The conversation might center on how she wants to practice rotating her wrist to the right. Although developing this very specific way of thinking takes years of mindful practice and attention, it is transformational.

A young woman, an executive determined to climb the ladder, consulted with me because she wanted to learn how to get her older supervisor to take her seriously. At first, she was too general, saying, "Well, there are some issues at work that have been on my mind and keeping me from improving my professional development."

That kind of language gives me zero information. I told her, "You need to know that nothing you say here leaves this room. You don't even have to tell me the person's name. I just need to understand the human interaction and context, so we can create a goal that's effective and will actually address some development you need. If you're too general, I can't help you."

Finally, she trusted me enough to provide me with examples of how her supervisor wasn't supporting her, how he was dismissive in meetings, and how, in those meetings, he checked his phone multiple times. I tried to help her do a mind shift and view that as a learning experience, especially if she wanted to build toward a leadership position. She needed to start recording her learning and what she learned from each of these experiences before she forgot them. Part of her goal was also to understand that person's personality the same way she would assess any audience.

You can modify your language and verbal and nonverbal communication style based on the personality of the individual you're addressing. One of the many ways to define communication skills is to categorize them as visual, auditory, kinesthetic, and auditory digital.

Visual communicators learn by seeing, and they frequently memorize information by looking at pictures. "I see what you mean," appeals to them more than "I hear you." Reserve that for auditory communicators who learn by listening carefully. Kinesthetic communicators learn by doing, and they often move and talk more slowly than other types. Although auditory digital communicators often exhibit characteristics of the other three communication preferences, they are most interested that messages make sense.[75] Like the func-

---

75 "Stop Conflict and Create Harmony in Business," Loyola Greyhound, November 4, 2017, https://www.loyolagreyhound.com/2017/11/.

tional type described below, they prefer steps, sequences, and well-thought-out plans.

For our purposes, let's look at analytical, intuitive, functional, and personal styles. You can find these in almost any corporate setting, and you'll have no problem recognizing them once you know what each type values.

The analytical communicator likes hard data and real numbers and may be suspicious of people who aren't in command of the facts and data. The intuitive communicator prefers the big picture, avoids getting bogged down in details, and cuts right to the chase. This person doesn't need to hear things in perfect linear order but prefers instead a broad overview. The functional communicator likes process, detail, timelines, and well-thought-out plans. This person communicates things in a step-by-step fashion so nothing gets missed. The personal communicator values emotional language and connection and uses them to discover not just what others are thinking, but how they're feeling. One style isn't better than the other. The key is matching your style to that of the person you're trying to reach.[76] In addition to being very specific about which particular CQ skill you are working on and when in the week you will work on it, you can amplify your transformation if you are able to adapt to the personality of the person you are communicating with. If you can then layer on what you learned about VI, you can take your development to the next level.

If you can then layer on what you learned about VI, you can take your development to the next level. Getting back to that young woman, I also pointed out that she needed to work on her vocal

---

76 Mark Murphy, "Which of These 4 Communication Styles Are You?," *Forbes*, August 6, 2015, https://www.forbes.com/sites/markmurphy/2015/08/06/which-of-these-4-communication-styles-are-you/#5a5cc3a3adb0.

image, including recording her voice, closing her eyes, and listening to how she sounded when that voice was her only method of communication. She was a smart woman—attractive, professional, and well groomed—but even on the telephone, when she called me, asking for directions to my office, she sounded like a little girl. So she had three major challenges: to be specific in identifying and setting her goals, to modify her communication style, and to improve her vocal image.

THE CQ SWITCH

My goal is not to *change* who you are. It is to *teach* you how to switch on who you really are. At this point, you have accumulated tools to transform each part of your communication message. Your CQ is now available to you on demand. You simply need to "flick your CQ Switch"; this is your superpower. It is your newfound, innate ability to turn on your toolbox of skills. This is the way you mindfully shift so that you are no longer stuck behind any self-limiting labels.

Change your internal voice. "I'm un-shy." Or "I am not in a state where I am ready to speak—yet." That voice should also reflect that you're fine if you don't want to speak in the moment, but you need to be able to access your checklist.

Once you change your label and realize it's not a definition of your personality, you'll develop confidence and shift your overall nonverbal communication. Even if you try to overcome it intentionally, it's so deep seated that it will still be whirling in your mind. That's when you need the switch.

If you are able to integrate the CQ growth mindset into your daily functioning, this will change your internal voice. For example, "I'm shy" will shift to "I am not in a state where I am ready to speak—yet." This then allows you personal space to implement the tools you have learned and seek opportunities to practice them. Once you reframe your personal labels, you'll develop confidence and shift your overall nonverbal communication.

When you need to remember who you are and that you are not a label, switch YOU on.

WHAT I WANT FOR YOU

I am on a positive path to help people—and, in fact, to help preserve the *human* in human contact—and I have seen my methods work for thousands. Still, if I can help even one person in this world overcome their fear and anxiety and find their voice, I will feel I have achieved my goal. Be that person.

Commit to moving beyond relaying information to influencing with your message. Commit to thinking about improving your communication skills to a daily intentional application of your CQ tools. Commit to adapting your message while being mindful of the neurochemistry of your audience to maximize your memorability factor. Commit to your personal transformation.

This is the time to think back to the beginning of this book, where I told you about the CQ puzzle. As we have learned, CQ is not formulated equally for nor developed in the same manner for all. CQ is bespoke to each of you. What you have learned throughout these pages are tools for you to connect as your personal CQ puzzle. As with any puzzle, you may not initially see how the pieces connect but when they all do, it is so satisfying to observe the final project. When you take a step back, you can see how it has all come together for you as an individual.

If you have read this far, you have the tools, and you have this book. You have the journal to help you plan when and how to use them. In the tracking journal you can download online, you'll be able to track what you need for each speaking interaction, whether public speaking, negotiating, networking, or even videoconferencing. Each time you check one off, you'll experience that great dopamine effect, so consider yourself popping a calorie-free chocolate truffle for each checkmark.

What's not to like about a chocolate truffle emotional gratification experience? It should be a win-win, right? Let me warn you about a possible pitfall.

All too often when I talk to potential clients about what they will need to do to change their vocal image and improve their communication intelligence, I hear the same excuse: "I don't have time." These exercises don't take much time. Most people do them while traveling to work or to an appointment, even driving to the grocery store. When I hear this excuse, I know that a potential client who cannot commit 250 seconds of his or her day to mastering communication intelligence—or who tells me, "I forgot to do the exercises"—has not set that mastery as a priority. I am calling on your geeky side—a CQ ethos is a must. Be proud of yourself when you complete your to-dos on your communication menu. Be tough on yourself when you do not and strive to do better next week. You are accountable to yourself. Push yourself to be a lifelong learner.

Make it your priority. Remember that the energy you give equals the energy you get. Check those boxes. Feel that dopamine. Then, one day, not so long from now, you'll be facing an audience, yet you'll also "be" in the audience, observing and monitoring yourself. And when you finish that speech, when the applause floods over you, and you stand there, awash in all those good feelings that come with accomplishment, and you don't see anyone reaching for a phone, you'll know the minimal time investment you made was worth it. You will actually feel the parts of your personal CQ puzzle come together. You'll recall that talk you just gave, moment by moment, and realize that you were in flow—and, yes, that you can do this again and again. You are indeed mastering communication intelligence. You have the tools!

Earlier, I mentioned how often people I work with realize it's not just them—that so very many with tremendous knowledge and talent are nervous and anxious when it comes to sharing their knowledge. So no, it is not just you, but I want you to know *it is within you* to realize the new path that will lead you forward.

In the final pages of this book on communication intelligence, we have journeyed through the captivating realms of human connection and understanding. We have explored the depths of empathy, the power of awareness, and the art of effective expression. Now, as we approach the end, let us take a moment to reflect on the profound impact that communication intelligence can have on our lives.

Communication, at its core, is the lifeblood of human inter-action. It is the bridge that connects us, transcending barriers of distance, culture, and ideology. Through effective communication, we can foster harmony, build relationships, and accomplish remark-able feats together. It is the force that propels us toward a future of endless possibilities.

Throughout history, great leaders, thinkers, and visionaries have understood the true essence of communication. They recognized that the quality of their relationships, the success of their endeavors, and the legacy they left behind were all intricately tied to their ability to communicate effectively. They understood that communication intelligence was not just a skill, but a catalyst for growth, innovation, and transformation.

Now, armed with the knowledge and insights gathered within these pages, it is your turn to embark on your own communication journey. You possess within you the power to make a profound impact, not only on your own life but also on the lives of those around you. You have the ability to inspire, motivate, and bring about positive change through your words and actions.

Remember that communication is a dance, a delicate interplay between speaking and listening, sharing and understanding. It requires patience, empathy, and a willingness to truly connect with others. In a world often overshadowed by noise and distractions, be the beacon of clarity and sincerity that illuminates every conversation.

As you venture forth, dare to be vulnerable, for it is in vulnerability that true connections are forged. Be present and fully engaged in each interaction, offering your undivided attention and genuine curiosity. Seek to understand before seeking to be understood, valuing diverse perspectives, and embracing the richness they bring.

In your pursuit of communication intelligence, you may stumble and encounter obstacles along the way. But do not be discouraged, for it is in those moments of challenge that your true strength emerges. Learn from each experience, grow from every interaction, and continue to refine your skills.

Remember that communication intelligence is not a destination but a lifelong journey. It is an ever-evolving process of self-discovery, self-improvement, and self-awareness. Embrace the growth mindset, always open to new ideas, feedback, and the possibility of transformation.

So as you close this book, may you carry with you the flame of communication intelligence, letting it illuminate every conversation, every connection, and every aspect of your life. May your words resonate with authenticity, empathy, and kindness, and may your actions inspire others to become champions of effective communication.

For it is through the power of communication intelligence that we can shape a world where understanding triumphs over ignorance, compassion conquers conflict, and unity surpasses division. The future is in your hands. Go forth and let your communication intelligence be the catalyst that propels you toward a brighter, more connected, and harmonious world.

Now your journey begins.

THE **CQ** EDGE

SIX-WEEK TRACKING JOURNAL

Contents

Introduction 1

CHAPTER 1
What Is CQ, and Why Do You Need to Master It? 3

CHAPTER 2
Mastering CQ 7

CHAPTER 3
Positive Psychology and the CQ Mindset. 11

CHAPTER 4
The Science behind CQ: Vocal Image 15

CHAPTER 5
The Physiology of Voice 23

CHAPTER 6
Cortisol and Stress—How to Control Them 27

CHAPTER 7
From Grit to Gravitas 31

CHAPTER 8

Your CQ Checklist—Content **33**

CHAPTER 9

Your CQ Checklist—Vocal Impact **47**

CHAPTER 10

Your CQ Checklist—Nonverbal Communication. **55**

CHAPTER 11

Next Step—Find Your Safe Place. **57**

Introduction

Through the activities that fill the following pages, you will master the concrete scientific formula behind CQ. Mastering it will enable you to:

- think quickly
- structure your speech clearly and sensibly
- craft persuasive language
- reduce the anxiety often triggered by speaking publicly or socially

To access more content complete your Tracking Journal online at www.subridgman.com! Let's get started on your CQ!

CHAPTER 1

What Is CQ, and Why Do You Need to Master It?

The first step toward speaking with communication intelligence is to take an honest look at ourselves and assess where we are.

One a scale of 1 to 10, 10 being the highest and 1 being "not at all": How confident are you?

SELF-ASSESSMENT	RATING	REASON
How would you rate your public speaking skills?		
How would you rate them in the context of speaking with your friends?		
What about when you're speaking in front of strangers?		
Coworkers?		
Superiors?		

SELF-ASSESSMENT	RATING	REASON
Do you really care about improving your public speaking skills?		
If you do have an inkling that you need to improve, where would you rate yourself now versus where you would like to be – aspirational number?		
How much effort are you willing to put in to achieve those results?		
Do you track your heart rate when in communication situations?		

If you made it past the third question, welcome! You have the self-awareness necessary to move forward and master intelligent communication. Since you've made it this far, let's get into more detailed questions.

SELF-ASSESSMENT PART 2

How would you describe your personality?

_____

_____

_____

_____

How would you describe your inner voice? Is it judging, critical, confident? What are the messages it sends to you?

_____

_____

_____

_____

Clearly define three of your personal goals for your communication skills development. For this purpose, a good goal is clearly defined and trackable, while a poor goal is too general and not easily tracked.

Examples of solid goals could include "to improve intonation, articulation, and mindfulness of my tendency to fidget when giving presentations at work" or "to be mindful of my tone and messaging during my next meeting with Person X, and to craft three messages I want to address the night before."

1. _____

2. _____

3. _____

Tracking Journal

WEEK 1 – PART I

Date _____

PUT IT INTO ACTION

REFLECTION

What did you learn about yourself after answering the questions above?

_____

_____

_____

_____

_____

_____

Are you ready to make a quantum jump in your CQ? Let's get started!

CHAPTER 2

Mastering CQ

The first step toward developing your communication intelligence is defining your vocal image.

We're going to look at how to step outside yourself and understand how to:

- consciously monitor your heart rate,
- control your breathing,
- observe your physiology,
- lower your stress response, and
- find easy ways to self-correct.

Once you achieve a high level of self-monitoring, you will be best able to access your brilliance! So how do you start on your own journey toward CQ? Let's answer a few baseline questions:

What are three speaking or communications situations when I get nervous?

1. _____

2. _____

3. _____

When I get nervous in one of these situations, I think/say the following to myself:

1. _____

2. _____

3. _____

What should I be saying to myself instead?

1. _____

2. _____

3. _____

Tracking Journal

WEEK 1 – PART 2

Date _____

PUT IT INTO ACTION

Record yourself on your smartphone. Listen to your voice. Try it slower, drop your tone. How does it sound to you when you do that?

_____

_____

_____

_____

_____

_____

_____

CHAPTER 3

Positive Psychology and the CQ Mindset

We all have a basic need to feel as though we've accomplished something. When we're rewarded arbitrarily, we lose motivation and consequently, happiness.

I invite you to be very specific and pointed in your goal setting. To have a measured awareness and positive feedback loop wherein you are cognizant of your progress, you need specific goals that are set, achieved, and tracked.

So, let's do a quick exercise—your personal check-in with respect to your current communication skills:

Self-Assessment Callout: Ask yourself seven questions with respect to your level of happiness and how it is being impacted by your communication skills.

SKILL	LEVEL	WHY?
How do I rate my personal communication skills at present?	_/ 10	
How do I rate my professional communication skills?	_/ 10	
How do I rate my confidence level?	_/ 10	
How much is my confidence level linked to my communication skills?	_/ 10	
How much is my happiness level linked to my confidence level?	_/ 10	
How much is my happiness level linked to my communication skills?	_/ 10	
How much is my nervousness level linked to my communication skills?	_/ 10	

Tracking Journal

WEEK 2

Date _____

PUT IT INTO ACTION

Take a moment to record your personal intention to shift toward optimism in regard to your communication goal and/or personality style that is impacting your communication skills.

What my mind is currently telling me about my personality:

_____

_____

_____

What I want my mind to tell me about my personality at the end of this developmental journey; what shift do I want to see happen:

_____

_____

_____

What my mind is currently telling me about my communication skills:

_____

_____

_____

What I want my mind to tell me about my communication skills at the end of this developmental journey; what shift I want to see happen:

_____

_____

_____

CHAPTER 4

The Science behind CQ: Vocal Image

Deepening our concept of image: What's your vocal image?

I have a big ask of you. I want you to expand your notion of the word *image*. I will take you through a four-step reflection activity as we explore the important concept of *vocal image*, which was introduced in chapter 2.

LEVEL 1: IMAGE

In the image that follows, use the blank lines protruding from the bubble to brainstorm what exactly the word *image* means to you. Use blue ink for this part of the activity and allow your thoughts to roam free. Feel free to add more lines as needed!

IMAGE

LEVEL 2: MY PERSONAL IMAGE

For this part of the activity and the next one, you will need two colored pens—blue and pink.

- Step 1: In blue ink, brainstorm ideas that come to mind when you think of what the phrase *personal image* means to you. For example, perhaps for you, it means being a persuasive speaker, being able to change people's minds and inspire them to action.
- Step 2: Also in blue ink, ask yourself the following questions, and write your reflections on "How do I view myself today? How would I describe my 'personal image'?"
- Step 3: In pink, write what you aspire your personal image to become; that is, your aspirational personal image.

PERSONAL IMAGE

LEVEL 3: MY PUBLIC PERSONAL IMAGE

- Step 1: Review those items you just brainstormed and listed. Turn your mind outward to *how you believe you are perceived by others*. Take a few moments to reflect on whether how you are viewed by others matches with what personal image means to you. You can think back, for example, to your performance reviews, moments of conflict, unsuccessful interviews/negotiations/pitches/meetings where the result was not aligned with your expectations. If you are unsure, you can ask your colleagues questions such as:

- How would you describe me as a person?
- How would you describe my presence?
- How would you describe my communication style?
- What are my communication strengths?
- What are my communication weaknesses?

- Step 2: Using the blue pen, write labels people may assign *you* based on their impressions. For example, you're a leader, you're assertive/submissive, you have an accent, you're young, you are promotional/deferential/accommodating. You can also include adjectives describing your mental acumen such as *wise, academic, intellectual, focused, smart*. And you can also assign labels based on your energy and temperament, like *calm, anxious, serious, lighthearted*. You might find that negative qualities make the list—*blunt, annoying, sarcastic*— along with descriptions broad enough to summarize your whole outlook: *positive, negative, hopeful, discouraged*.

With the pink pen, identify words you would *like* others to assign to you—your personal image goals—those you strive others to think of when they think of you. Examples include *confident, assertive, determined, focused, articulate, organized, detail oriented, kind, thoughtful, accomplished, respectful, bold*, etc. While the difference between Levels 2 and 3 may not be obvious at first, the distinction is important.

Level 2 is what the term means to you, both in general and in regard to your aspirations for yourself. Level 3 is *your* personal image—your impression of the labels others assign to you and your goals.

MY PERSONAL IMAGE

LEVEL 4: MY VOCAL IMAGE

We will soon delve into vocal image in much greater detail, specifically how to define and achieve yours. For the purposes of this activity, review the above and reflect. Did you include anything about your voice, your confidence, how people view you based on the verbal (language, tone, etc.) and nonverbal communication you use? Even among those who've considered the factors we outlined for the first three levels, it's easy to leave out vocal image. Many people fail to realize how important their choice of language, tone, pace, projection, articulation, and similar factors are in how they're perceived by others.

Using your blue pen, write your current vocal image. Tune into your present way of speaking by any means possible. If you're not well acquainted with your own vocal image, there are a number of things you can do to start seeing it objectively:

- Ask for feedback from family, friends, and colleagues whom you know to be constructive and honest.
- Listen to your voice.

- First, only audio. Listen to the quality of your voice. It sounds much different than what you are used to hearing, doesn't it?
- Next, move to video. Watch a recording of yourself the next time you give a presentation. Study it afterward in the way football teams study game videos to discover where they excelled and where they failed.
- If possible, review transcripts of your spoken words. While many components of vocal image—such as tone and pacing—can be best observed via recordings, reading a transcript may provide a better overview of your language choices. Looking at your speech in print can make things such as often repeated wording or "crutch phrases"—those phrases that don't serve the content of your speech but instead buy you a moment to transition to your next thought—stand out, when you may otherwise miss them.

Using your pink pen, write your personal goals—what you want your vocal image to become. If you're an awkward speaker, you probably want to emanate confidence and security. If you know you come across as reserved, you probably want to be perceived as being in your element and energized as you stand at the podium. If you currently worry about seeming monotonous and boring, it makes sense that instead, you want to engage your audience and present your material in a way that will excite them.

Filling out this part may be a breeze, especially if you are exceptionally self-aware. If you're having difficulty moving from the general thought that you'd like to improve and onto specifics, go back and consider the core features of a strong vocal image. Then branch out from each of these points.

Another approach you could take is considering the flip side of any present insecurities about your speaking style. If you're like many people, you have no problem picking out the faults in your vocal image. You may say that you're awkward, that you're too reserved, that you speak in a monotone, or even that you're boring. The good news is that these faults often unfold to reveal the very characteristics you would like to acquire and develop.

MY VOCAL IMAGE

Are you having trouble with the above? In case you are feeling stuck on this new concept, here are some questions for you to reflect upon:

Tracking Journal

WEEK 3

Date _____

PUT IT INTO ACTION

Refer back to the exercise in chapter 4 on pages 87 and 88. You can print multiple copies of this page so you can track how you shift over time. It is a wonderful introspective exercise that can help you track your progress!

	MY VI TODAY	MY ASPIRATIONAL VI	GOAL SETTING TIMELINE OR OPPORTUNITIES TO PRACTICE
MY COMMUNICATION STRENGTHS			
MY COMMUNICATION WEAKNESSES			

CHAPTER 5

The Physiology of Voice

As we continue to progress through this book, you will learn science-based tools, and each one will fall into one of these columns. Track your progress as you move closer to your most powerful vocal image by making notes about each tool you can apply, in order to maximize your skill set related to that specific communication message component. After you've put in time and practice with these tools, you'll find that you can easily apply them to numerous situations you encounter daily, including social contacts, networking situations, formal presentations, interviews, and even courtroom scenarios.

Tracking Journal

WEEK 4 – PART 1

Date _____

PUT IT INTO ACTION

EXERCISE 1: COUGH TEST—
FIND YOUR DIAPHRAGM!

The purpose of this exercise is to find your diaphragm and bring awareness to it so you can bring your breath from your diaphragm.

Imagine there is a balloon below your lungs. Place two fingers below your breast line and cough, as if you are trying to expand the area below your lungs. You will find the top of your belly move inward. That is where your diaphragm is.

Another way to locate your diaphragm is to pretend you are blowing up a balloon until you empty your lungs. With your fingers locate the part at the top of your abdomen which moves inward.

Do this daily this week!!!

Try to breathe from here for your breath exercises that you will learn later in this book.

EXERCISE 2:

For each of these columns, write your personal reflections on the current quality of each component of your communication message. Be observant of how you shift in your skills and track here by date. I am sure you will feel great pride when you see your progress over time!

Track this daily this week to see if you have any shift or greater awareness for each of these components.

DATE	7% CONTENT, STRUCTURE, VOCABULARY, PERSUASION ("WHAT YOU SAY")	38% INTONATION, ARTICULATION ("HOW YOU SAY IT")	55% NONVERBAL COMMUNICATION ("HOW YOU SAY IT")

SPEAKFLUENCE INTRODUCTORY ARTICULATION EXERCISES

Refer back to the exercise in chapter 4 on pages 87 oand 88. You can print mulitple copies of this page so you can track how you shift over time. It is a wonderful introspective exercise which can help you track your progress!

VIVALDI EXERCISE

MIND BODY AWARENESS — WHICH PART OF YOUR VOCAL PHYSIOLOGY IS ENGAGED WITH EACH SYLLABLE (TONGUE, TEETH, JAW, LIPS, UPPER BACK OF THROAT, LOWER THROAT, FRONT ROOF OF MOUTH, MIDDLE ROOF OF MOUTH)?

TRACKING — CHECK EACH TIME YOU COMPLETE BEFORE BEDTIME (25 SECONDS OF SPRING)

	DAY 1 (125 SECONDS)	DAY 2 (125 SECONDS)	DAY 3 (125 SECONDS)	DAY 4 (150 SECONDS)
	ba, bee bo, bye	ha, hee, ho, hye	na, nee, no, nye	ta, tee, to, tye
	ca, cee, co, cye	ja, jee, jo, jye	pa, pee, po, pye	va, vee, vo, vye
	da, dee, do, dye	ka, kee, ko, kye	qa, qee, qo, qye	wa, wee, wo, wye
	fa, fee, fo, fye	la, lee, lo, lye	ra, ree, ro, rye	xa, xee, xo, xye
	ga, gee, go, gye	ma, mee, mo, mye	sa, see, so, sye	ya, yee, yo, yye
				za, zee, zo, zye

DATE	SUN	MON	TUE	WED	THU	FRI	SAT
B							
C							
D							
F							
G							
H							
J							
K							
L							
M							
N							
P							
Q							
R							
S							
T							
V							
W							
X							
Y							
Z							

Mind Body Awareness descriptions:
- Back of throat
- Chest
- Middle tongue to roof of mouth
- Back tongue to back of throat (vs. C)
- Curling the Bottom tip of tongue to back of upper teeth
- Lips
- Front of tongue to front roof of mouth
- Lips (vs. M)
- Back of throat drop back of tongue and lips for the w, jaw
- Rolling tip of tongue to middle roof of mouth
- Front of tongue to front roof of mouth
- Tip of tongue to back of teeth
- Top teeth to bottom lip
- Lips together, tongue and jaw
- Back tongue to back of throat
- Back / mid of tongue to roof
- Mid tongue to roof and back tongue drop

Cortisol and Stress— How to Control Them

MINDSET IMPACT ON CORTISOL EXERCISE

Let's try an activity. I am purposely not giving you any context.

Grab a pencil and a timer. Use this speech bubble. Set the timer to forty-five seconds. (It is even better if you can ask someone to start the timer for you.) Once the timer starts, write as many words that start with the first letter of your name as you can. If you want to challenge yourself further, choose only adjectives or only nouns.

Great job! Now count the number of words you were able to place in the bubble. Ask yourself, did your mind go blank? Did you have any physical reactions when the timer went on? If yes, ask yourself why that might have been the case.

Tracking Journal

WEEK 4 – PART 2

Date _____

PUT IT INTO ACTION

REFLECTIONS:

Number of words: _____

Physical reactions I felt during this exercise:

_____

_____

_____

_____

_____

My mindset regarding completing this exercise:

_____

_____

_____

_____

_____

What worked and what I could have done better:

_____

_____

_____

_____

_____

This activity is very useful, as it triggers what happens to many in public speaking situations. There is a time limit, you have a message to share, and pressure is added. Despite it being a simple exercise, often clients say their minds go blank. This is because our bodies shut down, and "brain freeze" sets in when cortisol spikes. Mindset and cortisol release are interconnected. Control your mindset, use the exercises to control your cortisol release, and you will be off to a great start.

CHAPTER 7

From Grit to Gravitas

Grit develops with mindful intention. This week let us turn our minds to shifting our internal mindset (our inner voice) to using communication growth mindset language.

Each time you catch yourself using a fixed mindset phrase, stop, pause, breathe, and shift your language to be more growth-mindset driven.

DATE	SCENARIO	FIXED MINDSET PHRASE I USED	GROWTH MINDSET PHRASE FOR FUTURE

Tracking Journal

WEEK 5 – PART 1

Date _____

Let us refer back to the chart in chapter 7. See the examples below and insert an example of what you were about to say in column 2 and what you actually said in column 3.

GOAL	FIXED MINDSET PHRASE [WHAT YOU WERE ABOUT TO SAY]	COMMUNICATION GROWTH MINDSET PHRASE [WHAT YOU SAID]
Your mindset related to your confidence	E.g.: I must be the worse speaker on the planet.	E.g.: I may not be a strong speaker yet, however I'm a strong person for choosing to face this challenge.
Your mindset related to stressful situations	I got so scared I couldn't even think, never mind speak coherently.	I was surely overwhelmed in the moment, but I am so happy I remembered to use breath techniques I learned! That was better than last time.
The goals that you are trying to achieve in a communication context or opportunity	Everyone in the audience looks so much smarter than I am.	I am so impressed by the credentials of those in the audience, and honor myself for deciding to speak and share what I am passionate about. I deny the power of the voices in my head.
Kindness towards oneself when one doesn't achieve the goal intended	Well, that was a complete disaster.	Well, that was an excellent learning opportunity. While I feel much more confident in how I did X, next time I will...
A learning goal from each communication scenario that is presented	That could not have gone more horribly	What did I learn from this presentation? What did not work in this meeting? What reaction did I receive?

CHAPTER 8

Your CQ Checklist—Content

Here we'll go through some exercises that will enable you to build a winning presentation!

1. THE SPEECH BURGER

Mental visuals make for powerful reminders when you're in the moment. And just as the image associated with Ten Hook Fish can help you cue your audience immediately, the image of the speech burger can you help you maintain a clear, helpful structure. Use the graphic organizer below as you prepare your speeches or narratives.

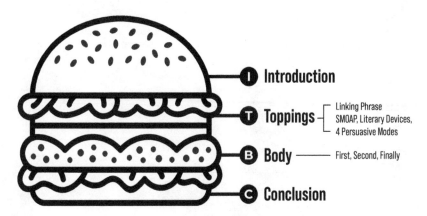

I Introduction

T Toppings — Linking Phrase
SMOAP, Literary Devices,
4 Persuasive Modes

B Body — First, Second, Finally

C Conclusion

In a speech burger, you have four main parts:

- top bun
- burger
- toppings
- bottom bun

The bottom bun is your introduction, including your hook and any introductory marks that build from that hook.

The meat is the bulk of the message—what the speaker is knowledgeable about. This is where you let your knowledge shine. When you begin, start with three main points.

The toppings are factors of speech such as similes, metaphors, onomatopoeia, alliteration, and personification.

This week, let's try to use the tools used to adapt your speech construction to be more persuasive and engaging.

Choose a random topic and write a speech that is two minutes long. Next, rewrite it using the suggestions below! These adaptations will transform the quality of your speech. If you are keen, repeat daily this week!

SPEECH BURGER STARTERS

Choose phrases from this chart to start building your speech.

<table>
<tr>
<td rowspan="1">TOP BUN: INTRODUCTION</td>
<td colspan="3">
Step 1: Hook
Step 2: What problem will be addressed, and what are you offering as a solution? If If an informative speech, what will be covered? Briefly—vision of the road map of your speech. Explain the salient idea (e.g., if you have ever wondered x, I invite you to learn with me today as I show you a new perspective of xyz).
Need to include some language examples where audience is convinced to give their attention for a certain amount of time.
<ul>
<li>My aim is that in the next twenty-five minutes you will transform your perspective on …</li>
<li>I will demonstrate to you today.</li>
<li>If x is what you are interested in, I invite you to sit, back, relax and enjoy the futuristic revelations I have to share with you today.</li>
</ul>
</td>
</tr>
<tr>
<td rowspan="1">TOPPINGS: DETAILS</td>
<td colspan="3">
<table>
<tr><td>· Signposting language</td><td>· Finally …</td><td>· Surely …</td></tr>
<tr><td>· Verbal punctuation</td><td>· Likewise …</td><td>· Certainly …</td></tr>
<tr><td>· First, second, third …</td><td>· Besides …</td><td>· Specifically …</td></tr>
<tr><td>· Furthermore …</td><td>· Again …</td><td>· If …</td></tr>
<tr><td>· In addition …</td><td>· Moreover …</td><td>· then …</td></tr>
<tr><td>· Also …</td><td>· Similarly …</td><td>· because …</td></tr>
</table>
Other toppings of speech
<ul>
<li>Simile: My love is like a red, red rose.</li>
<li>Metaphor: My love is a red, red rose.</li>
<li>Onomatopoeia: Over the rosebush, lightning flashed, and thunder roared.</li>
<li>Alliteration: Red roses remind Riley to remember and reflect.</li>
<li>Personification: The rose unfurled her petals and spoke words of love.</li>
</ul>
</td>
</tr>
<tr>
<td rowspan="1">BURGER: MAKING YOUR POINT</td>
<td colspan="3">
<table>
<tr><td>· For example …</td><td>· This should include examples of similes, metaphors, onomatopoeia, alliteration, pathos, logos, ethos, and Kairos.</td></tr>
<tr><td>· In fact …</td><td></td></tr>
<tr><td>· For instance …</td><td></td></tr>
<tr><td>· As evidence …</td><td></td></tr>
<tr><td>· In support of this …</td><td></td></tr>
</table>
</td>
</tr>
<tr>
<td rowspan="1">BOTTOM BUN: CONCLUSION</td>
<td colspan="3">
<table>
<tr><td>· For the reasons stated</td><td>· In short</td><td>· In brief</td></tr>
<tr><td>· As you can see</td><td>· To be sure</td><td>· Undoubtedly</td></tr>
<tr><td>· As I have noted</td><td>· Without a doubt</td><td>· In any case</td></tr>
<tr><td>· In other words</td><td>· Obviously</td><td>· To summarize</td></tr>
<tr><td>· On the whole</td><td>· Unquestionably</td><td>· In any event</td></tr>
</table>
</td>
</tr>
</table>

2. PERSUASIVE SPEECH

Consider your presentation. Decide which persuasive sentence structure best applies to your communication context and integrate the vocabulary into one of these structures.

PERSUASIVE SPEECH SENTENCE STRUCTURE	STEPS TO FOLLOW
1. Problem-Solution/ Opportunity	This structure involves identifying a problem and then offering a solution/opportunity. The goal is to convince the audience that your solution is the best one. The structure typically includes: · An introduction that establishes the problem and its significance. · A description of the problem, including evidence to support the claim. · An explanation of the proposed solution or opportunity. · Evidence to support the effectiveness of the solution. · A call to action, urging the audience to support the proposed solution. · Identify an opportunity for growth or progress in solving.
2. Monroe's Motivated Sequence	This structure is a five-step process that aims to motivate the audience to take action. The steps are: · Attention: Capture the audience's attention with a powerful statement or question. · Need: Present the problem and explain why it is important to address it. · Satisfaction: Offer a solution to the problem and explain how it will solve the issue. · Visualization: Use vivid imagery and examples to help the audience imagine the benefits of the proposed solution. · Action: Call to action, urging the audience to take steps to support the solution.
3. Comparative Advantage	This structure compares two or more options to demonstrate why one is better than the others. The structure typically includes: · An introduction that explains the context and importance of the comparison. · A description of the options being compared. · Evidence and arguments in favor of the preferred option. · Evidence and arguments against the other options. · A conclusion that summarizes the advantages of the preferred option.

PERSUASIVE SPEECH SENTENCE STRUCTURE	STEPS TO FOLLOW
4. Refutation	This structure involves anticipating and addressing counterarguments to your position and addressing them before presenting your main points. The structure typically includes: · An introduction that establishes the topic and its significance. · A description of the counterarguments and evidence against your position. · A rebuttal of the counterarguments with evidence and persuasive arguments. · A conclusion that summarizes the strengths of your position and weak points of the counterarguments.
5. Problem-Cause-Solution	This structure identifies the cause of the problem and then presents a solution. The structure typically includes: · An introduction that establishes the problem and its significance. · A description of the problem and its causes. · An explanation of the proposed solution. · Evidence to support the effectiveness of the solution. · A call to action, urging the audience to support the proposed solution.
6. Maslow's Hierarchy of Needs	Structure your argument around Maslow's hierarchy of needs, starting with the most basic needs (e.g., physiological needs) and building up to the highest needs (e.g., self-actualization).
7. Motivation-Action	Begin by motivating your audience to take action on an issue by highlighting the consequences of not acting.
8. Chronological	Present your argument in chronological order to show the evolution of an issue and the importance of your proposed solution.

You aren't just speaking words. You are creating pictures that help your reader experience your message.

Again, I will ask you to pause and bring awareness to the neurochemical impact words can have to affect our emotions and moods based on the sentence structure or syntax you use.

For your quick reference, consider the impact on your audience when you use any of these elements:

SENTENCE STRUCTURE OR SYNTAX	EXAMPLE	NEUROCHEMICAL IMPACT
Questions	"Have you ever wondered ..." or "How can we improve ..." "Have you considered ..."	Asking questions can create a sense of curiosity and engagement, which can trigger the release of dopamine and norepinephrine in the brain.
Repetition of words	"Yes, we can": Barack Obama's campaign slogan in 2008 "I have a dream": repeated by Martin Luther King Jr. during his famous speech. "We shall fight on the beaches, we shall fight on the landing grounds, we shall fight in the fields and in the streets, we shall fight in the hills; we shall never surrender": Winston Churchill's famous speech during World War II.	Repetition of words or phrases can create a sense of rhythm and familiarity, which can trigger the release of dopamine in the brain.
Contrast	"Ask not what your country can do for you, ask what you can do for your country ..." "Sometimes the greatest obstacles can lead to the greatest opportunities." "You can't appreciate the light without experiencing the darkness."	Contrasting ideas or phrases can create a sense of tension and resolution, which can trigger the release of dopamine and norepinephrine in the brain.
Metaphors and analogies	"Life is a journey, not a destination ..." or "She was a ray of sunshine." "She's a firecracker." "The world is your oyster." "Success is like a marathon, requiring endurance and persistence."	Using metaphors or analogies can create a sense of imagery and visualization, which can trigger the release of dopamine in the brain.
Positive affirmations	"I am capable of achieving my goals." "I am worthy of love and respect." "I am strong and resilient." "My voice matters."	Using positive affirmations can create a sense of self-confidence and motivation, which can trigger the release of dopamine and serotonin in the brain.

SENTENCE STRUCTURE OR SYNTAX	EXAMPLE	NEUROCHEMICAL IMPACT
Negatives	"I'm not saying it's going to be easy, but it will be worth it." "Not only did she overcome adversity, but she also thrived." "We didn't give up, and we succeeded."	Negative sentences can trigger the release of cortisol and create feelings of stress and tension in the brain. However, they can also be used to create a sense of contrast or to emphasize a positive outcome.
Inclusive language	"We can do this together." "Let's work together to achieve our goals." "Our team is strong and diverse."	Using inclusive language can create a sense of belonging and community, triggering the release of oxytocin in the brain.
Power words	"Revolutionary" "Inspiring" "Transform" "Conquer" "Empower" "Guaranteed" "Proven" "Exclusive" "Instant" "Sensational" "Incredible" "Phenomenal" "Unsurpassed" "Breakthrough" "Extraordinary" "Remarkable" "Authentic" "Powerful" "Elite" "Epic"	Power words can create a sense of impact and importance, triggering the release of dopamine and norepinephrine in the brain. Keep in mind that power words can be effective when used sparingly and strategically. Using too many of them can make the message come across as exaggerated or insincere. It's important to consider the context and the audience when using power words to create a persuasive message.
Direct questions	"What is your main goal right now?" "How can we work together to achieve our objectives?" "What is the most important thing you need to do today?"	Asking direct questions can create a sense of engagement and focus, triggering the release of dopamine and norepinephrine in the brain.

SENTENCE STRUCTURE OR SYNTAX	EXAMPLE	NEUROCHEMICAL IMPACT
Juxtaposition	"We have two choices: we can sit back and watch the world go by, or we can take action and make a difference." "The darkness of the night sky was in stark contrast to the bright lights of the city below." "The peacefulness of the countryside was a world away from the chaos of the city."	Juxtaposition: Contrasting and juxtaposing ideas can create a sense of surprise and novelty, triggering the release of dopamine in the brain.
Repetition of phrases	"Never give up, never give in, never surrender." "I can do this, I will do this, I am doing this." "It's not how many times you fall down, it's how many times you get back up." "Because you're worth it": L'Oreal's slogan. "Think different": Apple's campaign slogan in the late '90s. "I'm lovin' it": McDonald's slogan. "A diamond is forever": De Beers's slogan. "I want my MTV": A campaign to promote the launch of MTV in the early '80s. "Eat fresh": Subway. "The happiest place on earth": Disneyland's slogan.	Repeating key phrases or ideas can create a sense of emphasis and motivation, triggering the release of dopamine and norepinephrine in the brain.
Hypothetical questions	"What if we could create a world where everyone had access to education and healthcare?" "How would you design a product that solves this problem?" "If you had unlimited resources, what kind of impact could you make?"	Asking hypothetical questions can create a sense of curiosity and creativity, triggering the release of dopamine in the brain.

SENTENCE STRUCTURE OR SYNTAX	EXAMPLE	NEUROCHEMICAL IMPACT
Imperatives (Kairos)	"Take action now to achieve your goals." "Make a difference in the world today." "Never stop learning and growing."	Using imperatives can create a sense of urgency and motivation, triggering the release of dopamine and norepinephrine in the brain.
Personal anecdotes	"When I faced a similar challenge, here's what worked for me." "I once struggled with this issue myself, and I know how difficult it can be." "Let me tell you a story about how I overcame a major obstacle in my life."	Sharing personal anecdotes can create a sense of empathy and connection, triggering the release of oxytocin in the brain. Using a story to illustrate the benefits of taking a certain action or following a certain path can be very persuasive.
Descriptive language	"The sky was ablaze with a stunning array of colors as the sun set in the distance." "The aroma of freshly baked bread filled the air, enticing us with its warm and inviting scent."	Using descriptive language can create a sense of vividness and imagination, triggering the release of dopamine in the brain.
Rhetorical questions	"Who doesn't want to live a fulfilling life?" "Why settle for mediocrity when you can achieve greatness?" "Isn't it time we took action to create a better future?"	Asking rhetorical questions can create a sense of engagement and introspection, triggering the release of dopamine in the brain.
Alliteration	"Galloping gazelles graze on grass." "Wild winds whipped and whirled." "Ripe red raspberries roll around in a basket." "Purring Persian cats play with pink pillows." "A happy hummingbird hovers in the air."	Alliteration is a literary technique that involves the repetition of the initial sounds of words in a sentence or phrase. It is primarily used for stylistic purposes and can create a sense of rhythm, musicality, and emphasis in language. It can have an emotional and aesthetic impact on the audience when the brain processes language and appreciates the beauty of alliteration through the activation of various neural networks, such as the language centers in the left hemisphere and the reward centers in the limbic system.

3. MIND MAPS AND THE MEMORY TREE

A mind map is a simple way to visually structure and organize your ideas so that you can recall them at will and maximize your ability to be extemporaneous. Always remember that if you are relying on a script you are unable to fully focus on 93 percent of your delivery—because you are too busy reading. To reach peak performance I invite you to bear in mind this inversely-correlated relationship:

If your cognitive load is high, your performance will be low—If CL >, then P <

If your cognitive load is low, your performance will be high—If CL <, then P >

The mind map is important for these reasons:

- It bumps up your confidence.
- It improves your memory.
- It removes your dependence on a script.
- It helps you structure ideas.
- It decreases your cognitive load.

Mind maps have a central image that represents the key idea. Branches from the central image represent main themes. Each branch has a key word or image on it. Twigs off the branches represent details/ideas that are less central. All parts of the map fit together to reveal the key idea and its details.

You might choose to write out your script in advance. Then create colors as memory reminders. If you know that you want to slow down your pace at a certain part of your speech, use a certain color to indicate that. If you want to emphasize a certain word, maybe use a bright pink. Maybe you want to insert a purposeful pause. Once you highlight a written speech this way and read it many times, you will see those colors when you begin speaking.

Tracking Journal

WEEK 5 – PART 1

Date _____

PUT IT INTO ACTION

Volunteer to make a speech to your colleagues about something. It could be a new safety practice or process. Or just pretend and practice it anyway! Write it out below, using the Speech Burger method.

Remember, in a speech burger, you have four main parts:

- bottom bun,
- burger,
- toppings, and
- top bun.

The bottom bun is your introduction, including your hook and any introductory marks that build from that hook.

The meat is the bulk of the message—what the speaker is knowledgeable about. This is where you let your knowledge shine. When you begin, start with three main points.

Remember that the toppings are factors of speech such as similes, metaphors, onomatopoeia, alliteration, and personification.

MY SPEECH BURGER

BOTTOM BUN	
BURGER	
TOPPINGS	
TOP BUN	

Your CQ Checklist—Vocal Impact

The following exercises will help you understand where your voice originates from, and will show you how awareness and exercises will help you to further strengthen and control your voice.

FUPR (DETECTIVE)

Use this acronym I created to remind yourself to turn into Sherlock Holmes and do the following: Find your voice. Use your voice. Practice your voice. Refine your voice. You need to remember that you have four levels of voice, and you also need to understand your resonance and the quality of your voice.

TIGER

When I say four levels of voice, it is a guide to bring awareness and control over your volume and pitch. Think of a tiger finding its "roar"; analogize this to you finding your four levels of voice. I am surprised at how many people speak in a monotone and aren't even aware they possess vocal tools they aren't using. Sure, they can speak louder or quieter than their normal range, but they lack control. Here's an easy way to release your voice and learn about your vocal range.

Record yourself speaking while you plug your ears, then listen to the recording to hear the difference between what others hear and what you're hearing. Then try to assess what your voice is like. Visualize a ball. As you are throwing the ball higher, put more energy into your voice. Try to throw that ball up four levels—so, a little bit high, higher, highest, up to the ceiling.

THE PAPER EXPERIMENT

If I were to hand you a piece of paper and say, "Blow on this paper so that it makes noise," what would you do? Some people try to move it, but the easiest way to accomplish the task is to just blow really quickly on the edge of it. Then you will hear the noise of the vibration. This is especially effective as a group exercise. If one person is holding the piece of paper, and everyone is trying to blow on it, nothing will happen, because there isn't enough air aimed in the right direction. When one person takes the paper and blows aggressively on the edge, it results in vibration and sound.

The paper is symbolic of your vocal cords. You need to have air passing over them to get sound.

Another way to demonstrate this is with a balloon. Hold a balloon full of air to another person's ear and speak softly from the other side of the balloon. Your voice causes the vibration, which is a sound wave. The sound wave travels through the air to the balloon, through the balloon to the air inside the balloon, back through the other side of the balloon, through the air again, and into your partner's ear. You can hear the sound and feel the vibration through the balloon.[77]

---

77   "Science Experiment about Sound: Feel the Vibration," Teachers Pay Teachers, accessed January 25, 2022, https://www.teacherspayteachers.com/Product/Science-Experiment-about-Sound-Feel-the-vibration-1636554.

HUM BOOT CAMP

The purpose of this exercise is to bring awareness to which parts of your physiology you need to form specific syllables. So, for example, if you say the word "Ba," you will note that the burden of forming the syllable falls to your lips. If you say "Ca," you will feel the sound emanating from your throat. And it's possible to get even more specific. For instance, if you say, "Ca Ga, Ca Ga," you will realize that "Ca" uses the upper part of your throat, while "Ga" calls on the lower part. Learning to pronounce syllables properly is like muscle memory that your body engages on demand when you need it.

VIVALDI

For the exercise itself, you will say—sing, really—the first twenty-five seconds of Vivaldi's "Four Seasons Spring." You will do it using consonants, one at a time, with each vowel. So: Bah, Be, Bo, Bye. Cah, Ce, Co, Cye

This is an articulation exercise spoken to the music (which you can find online). A lot of people just go *ba, ba, ba, ba*. You need to have the lips touch. If you do this correctly, your mouth will get tired. Try for six syllables a day with a four-day rotation.

TONGUE SWEEP

Your voice is sometimes called the best instrument in the world because you can take it with you wherever you go. Just as you exercise other parts of the body, you have to learn to exercise each part of the body that creates the voice: tongue, teeth, jaw, lips.

Sweep your tongue across your teeth in the following patterns, six times each, ten times a day.

Sweep from your upper left molar to upper right molar. Then sweep from your lower right molar to lower left molar. Then, sweep from your lower left molar to your lower right molar, and finally, sweep from your upper right molar to your upper left molar.

TONGUE BOOTCAMP

Move your tongue to the front of your teeth and then to the back of your teeth. Then press it against the roof of your mouth and to the back of your throat, as far as you can go. Repeat ten times.

MASAKO MANEUVER

This was originally developed to help those with swallowing disorders. It will also help you. While placing the tip of your tongue between your front teeth, swallow.

THE YAWN

Holding your mouth as wide as possible, yawn for ten seconds.

TONGUE PULL

Stick your tongue as far out as you can. Then pull it in as far back as you can. Hold for two seconds.

CONSCIOUS SWALLOW

Swallow your saliva and at the same time, squeeze your neck and mouth muscles.

GAUZE SWALLOW

Holding a rolled-up cylinder of gauze between your front teeth, bite into it and swallow.

THE GARGLE

Placing your tongue as far back in your throat as you can, pretend to gargle.

TONGUE TWISTER

Press your tongue to the roof of your mouth and say, "Pass the pens and pencils, please," without using your tongue. This exercise will remind you that one needs to have the full physiology engaged to make each particular sound.

Then try to disengage your jaws: Open your jaw and try to say those words. You can't do it, can you? Finally hold your breath and try to avoid putting air into those words. It doesn't work. Many people don't realize that breath—air—is so important. This exercise will remind you that you need air to have sound.

THE BUS - ENERGIZE YOUR WORDS!

You want people on that bus with you (i.e., you want your message to reach them), and this tool will help you do that. It's a reminder of the importance of putting emotion into your delivery. Pretend you're a bus driver, and you can affect the people behind you with your voice alone. You can't turn around, and all they see is your back. When you're speaking, the energy you give equals the energy you get.

Here are four questions. Go ahead and speak them in an almost depressed tone of low energy.

- "Are you ready?"
- "Are you sure?"
- "Are you positive?"
- "Let's do it."

Now, repeat them finishing with a verbal question mark at the end - as if you are questioning yourself (lacking confidence).

Now, repeat them again quickly.

Finally, repeat them with lots of energy. Are you ready?

This is a fantastic exercise to prove to yourself that you can generate all this great energy just by changing your tone, articulation, and projection. Automatically, you can feel that you have completely transformed the energy level of people just with your voice, without access to any nonverbal communication, any facial expressions, even without content—with just four sentences that lack any significant meaning.

Tracking Journal

WEEK 6 – PART 1

Date _____

PUT IT INTO ACTION

Chapter 9 had many exercises to try on. Which ones did you find most useful?

What exercises did you try?

_____

_____

Which one did you like the best?

_____

_____

Why will it work for you better than the others?

_____

_____

CHAPTER 10

Your CQ Checklist—Nonverbal Communication

Date _____

PUT IT INTO ACTION

I USED TO DO...	NOW I DO...	IMPACT
Head Position		
Head Tilt		
Face		
Lips		
Smile		
Eyes		

Eyebrows		
Gesticulation		
Hands		
Palms		
Fingers		
Posture		
Legs		
Feet		
Body Movement		
Body Sway		
Online Appearance		

CHAPTER 11

Next Step—Find Your Safe Place

If you have read this far, you have the tools, and you have this book.

You have the tracking journal to help you plan *when* and *how* to use information I've given you.

You can also download the tracking journal online.

With this, you'll be able to track what you need for each speaking interaction, whether public speaking, negotiating, networking, or even video conferencing. Each time you check one off, you'll experience that great dopamine effect, so consider yourself popping a calorie-free chocolate truffle for each checkmark.

- Commit to moving beyond relaying information to influencing with your message.
- Commit to thinking about improving your communication skills to a daily intentional application of your CQ tools.
- Commit to adapting your message while being mindful of the neurochemistry of your audience to maximize your memorability factor.
- Commit to your personal transformation.

Make it your priority. Remember that the energy you give equals the energy you get. Check those boxes. Feel that dopamine. Then, one day, not so long from now, you'll be facing an audience, yet you'll also "be" in the audience, observing and monitoring yourself. And when you finish that speech, when the applause floods over you, and you stand there, awash in all those good feelings that come with accomplishment, and you don't see anyone reaching for a phone, you'll know the minimal time investment you made was worth it. You will actually feel the parts of your personal CQ puzzle come together. You'll recall that talk you just gave, moment by moment, and realize that you were in flow—and, yes, that you can do this again and again. You are indeed mastering communication intelligence. You have the tools now!

CONGRATULATIONS!

You have finished your 6-week Tracking Journal work and are ready to step into your power.

Be sure to check out my website at www.subridgman.com for updates, news and the latest research!